The Master Key To Handwriting Analysis

By Irene Marcuse

www.sunvillagepublications.com

The Master Key To Handwriting Analysis
By Irene Marcuse

SUNVILLAGE
publications

Cover design by www.WebCopyAlchemy.com

Historical Introduction

Preface

This book would not have been undertaken were it not for the many people in this country and abroad, who received my first volume, *Applied Graphology,* in a spirit of such friendship and appreciation. I am grateful for the support and encouragement extended to me by my private students and those who have taken my correspondence course. The demands of my many students and of ardent readers and their interest in the subject, have prompted this book and given me the incentive to delve even more deeply into the definitive side of graphology.

It gives me great pleasure to express my thanks to those persons who have helped me in the preparation of this book: To Dr. Otto v. St. Whitelock, who guided me in the structure of all the chapters, without whose help it would not have been possible for me to do this work; to Iris Jordan, my student and friend, for reading the whole manuscript and commenting on it; to my student, Ethel Sigoda, for helping in the preparation of the chapter on handwriting of the child; to Dr. Arthur Schaake, my student, for his research work; to Dr. W. Eliasberg, psychiatrist, for his many helpful suggestions.

The following chapters will gradually lead the reader toward understanding and interpreting the different features of handwriting, not only where the personal qualities of the writer are clearly expressed, but also where he tries to mask them behind affected mannerisms. Many features of handwriting will be interpreted by the reader as symptoms of conflict in his own mind. He will be led to solve his problems through a study of his own handwriting and will find many examples of such conflicting traits in samples of handwriting collected by the author during the many years of her experience. The samples will teach the reader to apply his newly won method in similar cases, and so gradually acquire experience of his own.

The author has endeavored to prove that nothing is surmise or mere intuition in graphology. On the contrary, each graphic trait will be explained in full detail in connection with the different combinations and associations. Only through those combinations can one do justice to the writer's personality in the analysis of handwriting.

CONTENTS

PART II-GREAT MUSIC-MASTERS AS PORTRAYED IN THEIR HANDWRITING

Contents

CONTENTS

PART I. SCRIPT PATTERNS AND GENERAL ANALYSIS

Historical Introduction

The first systematic attempts to study the relationship between handwriting and character traits were made in Italy at the beginning of the seventeenth century when Camillo Baldi published in Bologna a treatise presenting a method for judging the nature of a writer from his letters. Another book on the subject was also written by an Italian, Marcus Aurelius Severinus in the middle of this century. Both of these studies remained isolated attempts, however, and were apparently forgotten.

A new interest in handwriting arose a little over a hundred years later with Lavater's *Physiognomical Fragments,* published in 1775-1778. This book, which includes one chapter on handwriting, makes only dogmatic statements. Lavater expressed his thoughts in this way: "The stem of the letter, its height and length, the position of the letters, and the clarity of the writing reveal the writer's fertility of thought. If the whole handwriting looks harmonious, it is easy to say something about the harmonious character of the writer."

This, of course, was only intuitive interpretation. Goethe was also able to deduce the character of a writer by comparing his handwriting with that of others; a great collector of samples, he tried to find some basis of comparison. In a letter of 1820 he writes: "It is very complicated to find a way out of this labyrinth of different signs."

French Graphology. In France, a circle was formed for the purpose of studying the relationship between human qualities and their graphic expression. This group consisted of Cardinal Regnier, Archbishop of Cambrai, Bishop Soudinet of Amiens, and Abbé Flandrin, who became the teacher of Michon.

Abbé Michon made investigations into vast quantities of handwriting. Through his studies and observations, and with the help of his collaborators Dalestre and Debarolle, he collected the signs of almost every human quality. He published his system, producing an invaluable catalog of graphological signs and rules, based on his experience. He did not try, however, to connect the psychology of handwriting with other branches of psychology or physiology, or to form a theoretical system. It was Michon who coined the word *graphology.*

As a consistent endeavor, graphology started around 1860 in France with Michon, and was continued by his pupils. They tried to build up a strictly empirical interpretation of handwriting. If, in twenty handwritings of courageous people, they found a certain trait, such as an open "a" or a particular slant, they decided this was a trace of courage. This was the sign-age of graphology. To French graphologists, character was a mosaic of properties, each one related to a certain sign which could be removed or added to as one thought fit. Surprisingly, these Frenchmen were able to make good psychological diagnoses, probably because of their innate imagination and intuitive knowledge of human nature.

Graphological signs are by no means as antique as alchemy. In medicine, for example, graphological signs can be analyzed and combined as can any other group of signs. Generally, however, signs in medicine are not easy to interpret because they are only indirectly connected with the pathological process. Nevertheless, there are groups of signs in graphology. For instance, certain tremors in handwriting are indicative of Parkinson's disease or of general paresis. Schizophrenia can be noticed at first glance because of the characteristic graphic disorder.

Michon's disciple, Jules Crépieux-Jamin, abandoned Michon's doctrine of definite signs, and elaborated a system of co-ordination of dominant signs. In one of his books, he stated: "the study of elements is to graphology what the study of the alphabet is to reading of prose." He expressed the need for studying handwriting as an entity, and held that each trait contributed in varying degree to the interpretation of the whole. He also explained that graphology revealed the psychological and not the physiological personality. From his time on, graphologists have required knowledge of age and sex before undertaking a handwriting analysis.

German Graphology. A theoretical system of graphology based on psychology was the work of a number of Germans. One of these men was a handwriting analyst for a newspaper and drew attention to the subject by analyzing the script of its readers. A number of books and articles were published on graphology in Germany. A periodical on the subject was issued by a gifted woman, Rudolphine Pope, and by William Langenbruch. Medical doctors assisted in research. Dr. George Preyer was one of the most important physicians who published work on this subject. His *Psychology of Handwriting,* published in 1895, deals for the first time with the relationship of graphic movements to mental processes.

About 1890, there began in Germany a type of graphological work, which can be considered the beginning of a new method in analyzing handwriting. This new approach stressed the important fact that handwriting is dynamic, not static. It regarded the act of writing as an expressive movement, and handwriting as the objective record of this movement. The outstanding representative of this new approach was, besides the aforementioned Dr. Preyer, Dr. George Meyer who claimed that handwriting expressed the total individuality of the writer. Graphological signs, such as size and width of letters, t-bar crossings, i-dots, etc., no longer had a fixed meaning, but were interpreted as the result of a fundamental function, which might express itself in a variety of ways.

In 1897 another graphological periodical was founded by the young Hans Busse. The chief contributors to this magazine were Dr.

George Meyer, who was a psychiatrist, and Dr. Ludwig Klages, who overshadowed Dr. Meyer by his great work. It was Dr. Klages who developed a definite method for this new approach to the study of expression and thus founded a new system of graphology. He created a complete and systematic theory based on a conception of writing as a conflict between natural impulses and rhythm on the one hand and mental discipline on the other.

Dr. Klages asserted that each movement expresses itself in handwriting. For instance, the expression of joy puts one in an exalted mood; therefore it is reflected in handwriting by enlargement and speed. A sad state of mind slows down the tempo and diminishes the size of letters. He called this graphological law the "personal motive." Each person reveals his individuality in his own way, thereby influencing the individual rhythm in the formation of letters. The personal motive is not fixed, however. It changes with character development and is subject to the writer's external impressions. For instance, a rightward slant can become vertical by a change of character. On the other hand, we are aware of unconscious imitations, as in the hero worship of a son who identifies himself with his father and unconsciously imitates his signature.

The new aspect, which was elaborated in many volumes by Klages, gave graphology a scientific basis from which our progress dates. He founded the first graphological society in Germany as early as 1886, and raised this field of study to scientific acceptance. All present-day graphology with any claim to serving as a psycho-logical method is indebted to Klages, who was the first to formulate a general theory of expression. Apart from Klages, most of the outstanding work was done by Robert Saudek, whose important books were written in English during his stay in London.

The Swiss Dr. Max Pulver has contributed much important work on graphology in his books, *The Symbolism in Handwriting, Criminal Instincts in Handwriting,* and *Expression of Intelligence in Handwriting.* These three books are written in German, and up to the present have not been translated. Pulver pointed to new possibilities in the interpretation of graphic traits. He has done pioneer work in demonstrating how both conscious and unconscious drives are projected in the writing pattern.

Pulver enlarged and modernized the graphological findings of Klages. Of great importance for graphology have been his investigations of economic crimes as outlined and discussed in his book, *Criminal Instincts in Handwriting.* Through his penetrating analyses of the handwritings of internationally known financial criminals, he proved the practical importance of graphological collaboration in cases of embezzlement and industrial crimes. As a student of Pulver, I have, among other fields in graphology, specialized in criminal investigations, which will be discussed in Chapter 11.

Another author of great importance to the development of graphology is Hans Jacoby. He has given us some of the best books written in English on the subject. Jacoby's works contain many specimens of handwriting with analyses, demonstrating what can be done with graphology to help solve human problems.

American Graphology. The influence of France and Germany is evident in American Graphology. Graphology in the United States owes its first investigation to Louise Rice, who founded the American Graphological Society in 1927.

Experiments of expressive movements based on handwriting were conducted at Harvard University by Gordon W. Allport and Philip Vernon in 1930-1931. These men based their investigations on three assumptions: (1) personality is consistent; (2) movement is expressive of personality; and (3) the gestures and other expressive movements of an individual, such as gait, facial expression, etc., are consistent with one another. Allport and Vernon published their findings in 1933 under the title, "Studies of Expressive Movements." To quote from their paper: "Continental psychologists see in graphic movements the quintessence of expression. It is a crystallized form of gesture, an intricate but accessible prism which reflects many, if not all, of the inner consistencies of personality... Handwriting provides material that is less artificial than tests, and more convenient for analysis; and since it can be studied at leisure, it is superior to facial expression, gesture, and gait, which are so fleeting and difficult to record. . . No one who has considered carefully the experimental and theoretical work on handwriting seems to deny the *a priori* case for graphology. Graphic movement apparently is not activity that is dissociated from the complexities of personality; on the contrary, it seems to be intricately woven with deep-lying determinants of conduct. Graphic movement is, therefore, expressive movement. If our thesis is correct that expressive acts are not specific and unrelated to one another, then handwriting itself will show consistencies with other expressions of personality." Robert Saudek participated in these experiments. He was the editor, until his recent death, of the first serious American periodical in the field of psychological graphology, now appearing under the title *Character and Personality,* published at Duke University.

Among the most recent contributions is Werner Wolff's *Diagram of the Unconscious,* Werner Wolff is one of the contemporary authorities in the field of experimental graphology, and his book is the result of many years of research and observation. A still more recent publication is Ulrich Sonnemann's *Handwriting Analysis.* This is a comprehensive volume, contributing much to clinical graphology. Klara Roman has written an excellent book, *Handwriting, A Key to Personality.* Other excellent books are A. A. Roback's *Personality,* and Gardner Murphy's *Personality.* My own first volume, *Applied Graphology,* was published in 1945. All of these books have aroused interest in the scientific analysis of handwriting.

/.

Uses of Graphology

Graphology is the scientific study of character expression in handwriting. It starts with the psychology of personality. The personality manifests itself in every kind of human expression, especially in those infinitely fine movements of the hand which guides the pen. Movements point to certain urges, and it is this combination of urges which may be found in handwriting, as distinct from the purely motive power.

To give an example, if one finds a stiff, angular handwriting,

Boston – to three
any way to study
Graphology here

one immediately gains the impression of stiffness. But is it not possible that this is a personality which, with the utmost energy, was able to bridle a rich emotionalism? And if so, why did the writer think he must overcome this inner warmth? Or is this writer primarily a volitional type, with no emotional temptations to hold in check? The problem which must be solved in each graphological diagnosis is: direct expression or inhibition? Co-operation or antagonism? One must not forget that every personality lives in a social world, has his social contacts, and meets with social encouragement or prohibition. To do justice to the writer in each case, one needs a rich experience of life and intuition, as well as scientific knowledge of the varying characters, attitudes, and dispositions of people.

It is difficult for graphology to reach into the past. Only if one is so fortunate as to have very early samples can one follow the development of a personality and venture an historical diagnosis.

Graphology definitely cannot establish the span of life. It can foresee, with a considerable degree of accuracy, the proneness toward suicide or accidents, especially in collaboration with neurology, psychiatry, and industrial medicine. In short, graphology is the visual dramatization of the present movement of the personality.

In Europe, graphology has reached the stage of being taught as a science in universities. In Germany, the Universities of Hamburg and Freiburg teach graphology. In France, it is taught at the Sorbonne in Paris; in Switzerland in Zurich, Berne, and Basel. Already Crépieux-Jamin has interested Binet in employing graphology for his famous tests, and Binet has used graphology regularly.

In the United States graphology is taught at The New School for Social Research in New York City, and at Boston University. American universities and colleges are becoming more interested in graphological problems. Graphologists of reputation are asked, on various occasions, to co-operate with investigators in psychological laboratories and to lecture before students. I have been invited to lecture at Yale University before a group of medical students and psychiatrists, and also before the staff at several mental hospitals. New York University has invited me to lecture on vocational guidance to students of social science. From my own experience I might say that handwriting analyses have been authenticated by the corresponding exactness of graphological findings. A certain amount of intuition is nearly always necessary in the formation of an analysis, but the groundwork must be applied first from actual objective observations gained as a result of close investigation.

The services of handwriting analysis are used for vocational guidance and for diagnoses of personality. Such service has proved its value in the definite placement of persons suited to positions in business. This subject is elaborated on in Chapter 8. The following is an expression of the attitude of an American company, The Pacific Weavers Corporation of New York City: "We have used graphology in our business for more than twenty years, here and abroad. Analyses have been of great advantage in screening personnel, for by placing the right person in the proper position one gets more work from fewer employees. We use this method for all workers; it works as well with the white-collar workers as with the mechanics. Graphology has also proved to save time, money, and trouble; it eliminates interviewing people unsuited for the position."

Psychology, neurology and psychiatry are the fields in which graphology can directly contribute to diagnosis, because here we are dealing not so much with graphology as with the aspect of what the graphic disorder reveals. A psychiatrist's evaluation of graphology is given by Dr. Hector J. Ritey of the American Board of Psychiatry: "Handwriting analysis has a definite advantage over every other projective technique, inasmuch as the patient is completely unaware of the fact that he is undergoing a test while writing. The patient does not know the meaning of the technique of the Rorschach or T.A.T. tests, either, but he knows that it is a psychological test, and his response consciously or unconsciously may be influenced by such awareness. But when one writes, one's attention is concentrated *on what* one writes, and not on *how* one writes. The movements of the hand are completely automatic and not subject to conscious factors."

The Manhattan Children's Court and King's County Hospital in Brooklyn, all in New York City, employ handwriting analysts as clinical consultants in treatment. For practical reasons graphic disorders are treated in many graphological texts. I have gone into this subject in Chapter 10. In mental hospitals, handwritings are gathered and compared to evaluate the effect of treatment. These investigations are especially useful in cases of the criminally insane, as is borne out in this statement of Dr. William Perl, psychiatrist in the military prison at Fort Leavenworth, Kansas: "I evaluate the prisoners as they come in and they are given a battery of standard psychological tests. I also study and analyze the handwriting of every prisoner as part of my routine evaluation procedure. I find it particularly valuable in judging such traits as impulsiveness, emotional stability, planning, concentration, ease with which a man might be influenced, and for recommending the man for a parole, clemency, restoration to duty—or nothing at all. I find handwriting anlysis as part of the over-all data most valuable in this undertaking. In 1951 I started here a group psychotherapy program and I am now engaged in the study of personality changes after group therapy which was conducted in a prison setting of the type we have here. For this study of evaluation changes after group psychotherapy, I am using handwriting analysis, too, as part of the over-all psychological evaluation procedure."

During World War II psycho-graphological analyses were officially used by the army both in the Military Intelligence Service and in vocational guidance by a number of psychologists trained in this particular method of personality evaluation. One of these psychologists, Herry O. Teltscher, served as a member of the Military Intelligence Division of the War Department at an installation where handwriting analysis was utilized for the purposes of character analysis. So successful was this approach that, at the end of the war, Teltscher was awarded a citation for his services by the commanding general of the Military Intelligence Division.

Handwriting analysis served still another purpose during the last war, that of vocational and educational guidance in one of the largest army hospitals for neuro-surgical casualties, the Thomas M. England hospital in Atlantic City. Teltscher was assigned to the reconditioning department of the above institution where his analyses were employed during the process of vocational and educational counseling of amputees and brain-injured patients. The graphological analyses were frequently coordinated with data obtained by the interview method in order to arrive at objective evaluations of existing potentials and the possibilities of vocational and educational training.

Whatsoever a man does, feels, senses or thinks will leave an imprint on his individuality. Since handwriting is one of the most important expressions thereof, the individuality must be reflected in the formation of each letter and word, relating to its cause and motivation.

Grand and eloquent gestures, when found together with a rightward slant, reveal a generous approach toward others: the "I-to-you" movement. Such writers are more prone to mix with people than are those who write a backward slant characterized by small and narrow traits. The first style of writing is, in most cases, attributed to the extrovert; the second to the introvert, who turns inward to himself and is satisfied to work or be alone.

Soft and gracious movements with large and rounded letters reveal the affectionate person who tends to avoid struggle and conflict, but likes to fit in smoothly; by contrast, the writer with angular connections is prone to fight for his goal and to overcome obstacles. The sharp movement resulting in angularity discloses also the writer's consistent working habits and endurance, as well as stubbornness and rigidity of feeling. The letter with a rounded top, which is almost a concealing stroke, belongs to the person who will not come out into the open but will try to cover his actions behind a front of artificiality. The threadlike connection gives the impression of running away. This also shows that the writer is evading something; at one time he cannot face himself, at another he cannot avoid breaking any promise because of his weak or evasive character.

The three zones also give us a good picture of the writer. The middle zone, or basic line, is the zone of the small letters on which the whole handwriting rests. If steady, in addition to being regular, we know that the writer is emotionally and mentally stable. If it wavers a little, this does not mean that the writer will possess instability, but that he will be more easily influenced than the one with a steady basic line. If, however, this line is uneven, in addition to exhibiting a conspicuous change in the size of small letters, we are sure that we have to deal with an unstable person whose actions and thoughts are incoherent. Exaggerated extensions of the upper and lower zone often corroborate this fact. The normal emphasis on the upper and lower zone shows the well-balanced person, with either intellectual, artistic interests (upper zone) or material and earth-bound ones (lower zone). The lower zone is considered the ground on which we stand, and each well-balanced person should exhibit a normal length of lower and upper loops.

If letters are well-knitted together, especially in a small script, we know that the writer will properly take care of all the details in his work. If, on the other hand, letters are illegible and loose, or can be mistaken for other letters, the writer will be careless and not responsible.

Any change of slant is very revealing because if one directs oneself steadily, the slant will be either consistently to the right or to the left, or standing up straight. If the writer slants in all directions, he is weak in purpose and scatters his abilities; this generally results in complete distraction. In a favorable case it discloses versatility, but then the whole writing must show a steady basic line and no divergence in the size of letters.

With the exception of the ten invariable traits shown on page 35, the fact that several meanings are given one sign does not indicate vagueness and uncertainty, but rather discriminating distinction. Sign validity has, of course, been determined empirically by experienced graphologists observing one graphic feature in millions of successive script patterns wherein it combines logically with many other traits. The psychological meaning conveyed by a single graphic quality such as "narrowness" covers a large number of simultaneous applications to specific characteristics, of which only a few are invariable. "Fear" is such a one. There are other indicators which are interdependent. They are ambivalent, varying from an extremely negative meaning to such a positive one as "self-control."

Determination of the exact meaning in terms of personality value, conveyed by either single or combined graphological indicators, is dependent primarily upon the writer's sense of value contained in the handwriting itself, e.g., on its level of form quality.

Another indicator which can be interpreted in various ways is "tempo and fluency." If these traits are combined without any rhythmic disturbance, irregularity, or uneven basic line, they must be interpreted as quick thought and good perception. In the opposite case it will mean "flightiness, lack of concentration, and general lack of balance."

Pressure, for instance, is understood generally to indicate some concentrated energy for work, varying according to the degree of pressure. This assumption would set up a scale for the quantitative measurement of pressure. The result of this assumption may mislead the investigator, because ignorance of indicators modifying this assumption would result in a concept far too general to correspond to any positive quality of personality.

However, it must be emphasized that, preceding the systematic analysis of any sample of handwriting, the examiner must focus upon the sample as a whole, totally ignoring the message and allowing the script to turn into a pattern of movement. This phase of investigation not only affords the examiner an over-all impression of the sample, but also allows single or recurrent characteristics to catch his attention. This same method is employed again at the end of the investigation where it serves to restore a proper and total frame into which the various data of observation can be fitted. Otherwise, the relative characterological significance of the personality may become lost in the process of concentrating upon single graphic details. The point to be emphasized is, that we must not try to determine single traits but personality as a unit. This personality unit can be the proper objective criterion against which to check graphological findings.

This method does not exclude the graphological examination of personality with regard to specific traits, but it certainly does obviate any direct and isolated graphological judgment of single traits. Judgments of this kind must be inferred from the whole personality structure and must not be based on isolated qualities of handwriting interpreted outside of their given texture.

It follows that procedure in graphology should be carried out on the level of evaluation of the entire personality rather than on the level of any specific presumed interpretative assumption, that the reader has studied and absorbed the whole technique presented here, and is equipped to apply the rules correctly as a tool in the combination of different traits.

As with all modern techniques and sciences, one must undertake a course of study and acquire a considerable degree of skill and understanding before one can hope to practice, or even to understand, graphology and its proper applications. As with law or medicine, one must understand the meaning of many basic terms, comprehend the method of approach, and acquire some knowledge of objectives and possibilities before undertaking even the simplest diagnosis. As in the study of disease, individual signs may have great or little significance; most often, they must be combined with all other known characteristics to present a clear and accurate picture.

Anyone interested in the serious study of the subject must, therefore, be prepared to apply his mind to the information given in the various chapters of this book and assimilate it as a preparation for a thorough understanding of the case histories which follow. To do otherwise—to skip to the heart of the book without first comprehending basic principles—would be equivalent to attempting to diagnose some physical infirmity without even a rudimentary understanding of physiology.

2.

Technique of Graphology

Anyone knows from his own experience that his handwriting varies if at one time he uses a soft, broad nib and at another a stiff, pointed one; that when exhausted and tired he writes otherwise than when well rested and fresh. There may be many other varia-

These two samples were written by the same person, the upper when tired and exhausted and the lower when rested and fresh.

tions. Therefore, without knowing the circumstances under which a handwriting has been produced, we cannot make allowances for all those factors which might have affected the fluency of the writing.

To the expert, all the circumstances under which the test was written are as clearly revealed as if he had sat opposite the writer and watched the minutest movements: his posture at the desk, the way he placed the paper in front of him, the firm or loose grip of the pen and its upright or sloping position, whether a broad or pointed nib was used, and whether the ink was fluid or heavy. All these factors are betrayed in the traces left by the pen upon the paper.

The graphologist has learned to recognize under the microscope the presence of such incidental circumstances. To the enlightened observer, the handwriting reveals also the school copy from which the writer, as a child, learned to write. It also shows whether he has lived for some time in a foreign land and consciously or unconsciously adopted some traits native to that country. His handwriting, furthermore, reveals his memory for forms, for it alters not only with his character development, but also with all those visual impressions stored up in his mind.

The following, then, are the individual characteristics which the trained graphologist studies when he undertakes an analysis:

Pressure

Genuine pressure is executed by the writer's own strength forced on the writing material by the pen. We must distinguish between heaviness of pressure caused by the actual strength of the writer and the mechanical heaviness resulting from a soft pen. Generally an adult chooses a pen according to his special way of writing. When a sample of handwriting is submitted for analysis, we assume that the writer has chosen the pen which suits him best and that the sample is fluently and naturally written.

Heavy Pressure

The principal and proper place for the application of pressure is on the down stroke, expressing the core of the personality, as in the "g" and "y" in this sample. The degree of pressure can be computed by measuring the diameter of the up and down strokes. Max Pulver applied the all-inclusive term "libido" to the various degrees

Hoping, that you are well and busy,

of shading in the genuine pressure. Heavy pressure is naturally used by the vital and energetic writer, as well as by those unskilled in writing. All persons of physical and mental strength who are active and possess driving power and energy display a proportionately heavy pressure in their scripts.

course in handwriting

Light Pressure

Light pressure can be produced by gliding over the paper with the least possible effort; it therefore indicates lack of driving power and sexual urge. The writer who uses light pressure seldom has a strong constitution and has little strength for combating life. He is easily influenced by the world around him.

reading your book on Graphology and enjoye

Pasty Pressure

Pasty pressure has no dark and light gradations in the up and down strokes. The pen travels over the paper without any distinct shading. Those who are motivated mainly by physical pleasures write in this manner. Pasty pressure is used by those who are impressionable; we find this pressure in the handwriting of artists. It should be noted that pasty pressure, which is characterized by evenness of stroke, can in addition be heavy or light, according to the writer's force or lack of it. The writer with heavy pasty pressure will never leave the sensual world for the spiritual one. He acknowledges the power of all sensual instincts and is especially prone to overemphasize this side of life. Originality is expressed in pressure. In the handwriting of the creative mind the pen seems to penetrate the paper. This individual shading gives the writing a perspective called the third dimension. The more apparent this perspective quality is, the stronger is the writer's creative imagination. This difference in shading can be observed in the handwriting of the genius.

Horizontal or Displaced Pressure

We often encounter horizontal or displaced pressure. This special phenomenon is a systematic displacement of the normal pressure from the down stroke to the side stroke. In this sample, the downstrokes of the "y's" have a tendency to shoot over to the right; what should be vertical strokes in the "i's" and especially the "d" show this tendency in exaggerated degree. On the constructive side, such displacement of pressure reveals that the sex drive is sublimated and harnessed so that it leaves one free for creative work. We see marked evidence of this dynamic phenomenon in the handwriting of the genius. This type of pressure reveals a displacement of the libido in cases of sexual maladjustment. Since we identify pressure with libido, this displacement of pressure can stem from different causes. However, it is never quite natural. Physical and mental strength, which in the natural process of growing up are meant to be developed equally, are not properly balanced, resulting in the transposition of the pressure to the side stroke. Disturbances of different kinds, especially mental abnormalities, are often found in the horizontal pressure. In such cases the pressure will be uneven.

Smeary and Muddy Pressure

This sample shows smeary pressure in addition to some peculiarities which reveal emotional and physical disturbance in the writer. This smeariness is especially evident in the "o," "n," and "d" of the word "correspondence." A muddiness in the pressure discloses

your Modernized Correspond- ence Course in Graphology

mental imbalance. A smeariness reveals the writer's addiction to alcohol.

anyway I would like more information about it

Please send me the time to investigate it. Now while I'm still

Uneven and Wavering Pressure

Uneven and wavering pressure shows indecision, unsteady will power, and lack of any purpose in life. The writers using such pressure are often changeable in mood and unreliable in character. They are prone to harbor petty jealousies and are seldom carefree, but instead are always worrying about troubles and ailments. Wavering pressure is characterized by a general irregularity and uncertainty; uneven pressure can be detected by the uneven flow of ink.

information regarding you course in graphology or

Basic Line

The basic line is a mirror of the emotional faculty. As the direction of the basic line varies, so does the writer's control of his emotions. In cases of an absolute straight line, as in the above sample, we know that the writer's mind dominates his emotional life. When in doubt about whether the line is even, turn the page upside down; this gives a clear indication of evenness. There are certain deviations from the even basic line, which we call a wavering line and an uneven basic line. These can be noted in samples on page 29 of wavering and uneven pressure.

about your analysis.

Regularity

Absolute regularity is seldom encountered in any writing because whatever is produced by man is variable. There are, however, degrees of regularity; this means that a certain arbitrary size is maintained in the distance of up and down strokes of the small letters. In this sample, for instance, the three "a's" are remarkably similar in size and stroke. Regularity of movements of the pen discloses a capacity for work and concentration. An equal height and width of letters gives evidence of perseverance, physical resistance, and consistency. When regular writing is coupled with angularity, it shows some rigidity of feeling and little adaptability to circumstances.

Irregularity

Irregular writing, in addition to uneven pressure reveals instability of emotions and inconsistency of character. We find irregulari-

'Sincerely Yours,

ty in the handwriting of artists and other creative minds. However, in this case irregularity is complemented by individual letter forms.

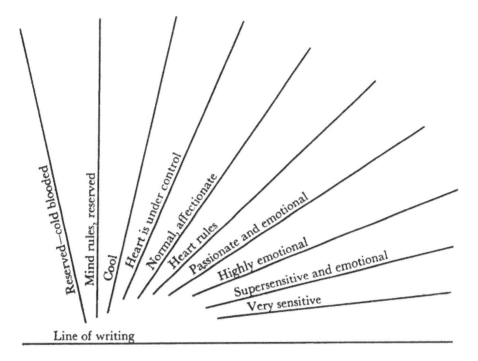

Line of writing

Slant

This diagram shows the degree of affection, emotion, and sympathy in the writer. The degree to which the handwriting slopes indicates the qualities in question.

Medium degree of rightward slant:

Sincerely yours,

The rightward slant discloses initiative, activity, and an interest in the world and its demands. When used with rounded and grace-*High degree of rightward slant:*

Credo" from kidli's

ful letters, an enterprising and progressive mind and a sociable nature are revealed.

Vertical:

interested in graphology. Would

Vertical handwriting indicates reserve, self-command, and a lack of spontaneity. The writer usually is a person with a critical nature, whose mind rules his emotions.

Leftward slant:

Dear Mrs. Marcuse

The leftward slant symbolizes reserve and also fear for the future. We find this slant often in the handwritings of adolescents. In the adult we recognize this as an expression of a reserved attitude, bordering on an attitude of self-defense, which often follows disappointment.

Continual change of slant:

Please send me

Change of slant discloses a moody and erratic nature. We find change of slant in the writing of people who are versatile and adaptable.

Tempo and Speed

In order to ascertain speed in writing we must determine whether the strokes are smoothly and firmly executed. Speed can be recognized where the writing runs on without interruption and is energetic and flowing. Rapidity means activity; an active mind always writes fast.

Fast

the capacity

kindly let me know what

Hasty

This sample is slowly written, with great care in dotting the "i"

like to have

exactly in the center. The t-bar also is placed in the center of the stem, revealing the slow tempo. Slow scripts, leftward and narrow, with exactly dotted I's, betray the hesitation of a writer who procrastinates. He who writes slowly is usually slow and cautious in his actions and reactions. The introvert often writes slowly, while the extrovert tends to write rapidly. To detect the tempo is not easy for the beginner. It is advisable to go over the writing with a dry pen, thus obtaining a feeling of the tempo in the writing movement. Pressure, basic line, regularity, and tempo indicate the writer's innate constitution and temperament.

Three Zones

Handwriting is divided into three zones: the upper, middle, and lower. In this diagram, the small letters such as i, e, r, m, n, etc., represent the middle zone; letters containing lower extensions such as g, p, j, y, etc., form part of both middle and lower zone. Letters such as 1, b, t, and especially the capitals, extend into the upper zone.

	Upper zone
Eternity	Middle zone
	Lower zone

In this sample, the writer's tendency to raise so many letters

into the middle zone discloses the writer's intellectual and spiritual life, his imaginative powers and creative ideas.

In the next sample the writer concentrates most of his letters in the middle zone which expresses the conscious, unimaginative, everyday life. The writer's intelligence and his capacity to adapt himself to circumstances are revealed in the formation of the small letters.

The writer of the next sample strays so deeply into the lower zone, as in the two "y's," that he betrays not only the material and physical life, "sensuality," but also his tendency to recede into his subconscious life and the world of his dreams.

kindly forward

There is often a good distribution in all zones, disclosing the writer's balance in all interests. Here the "k," the "d," and the "1" are carried high into the upper zone, but this is balanced by the equal drop of the "y" and the "f" into the lower zone and the regularity of the small letters which concentrate in the middle zone.

Although graphic traits often have different meanings in various combinations in scripts, there are some basic graphic traits which remain constant in whatever type of writing they are found.

These we shall call "invariable traits" and enumerate them:

1. SPACING:	Even: clearness of thought. Uneven: confused.	
2. ZONES:	Balance between three zones: a balanced person. Disproportion: imbalance.	
3. FLUENCY:	Quick, alert and connected thought.	
NOT FLUENT:	Slow, hesitant.	
4. INITIAL STROKES:	(After the writer's 25th year): Dependency on past experience.	
No INITIAL STROKE :	Independence.	
5. BASIC LINE:	Even: emotional balance. Uneven: emotional imbalance.	

(Continued on page following)

(List continued from prior page)

6. REGULARITY: Consistent working habits.

    IRREGULARITY :   Inconsistent.

7. SMALL LETTERS :   Defined: clear and concise thought.
                             Undefined: muddleheaded.

8. VERTICAL SLANT: Mind controls emotions.

    NON-VERTICAL SLANT :   Emotions dominate mind.

9. EVEN PRESSURE :   Healthy in mind and body.

    UNEVEN PRESSURE :   Ailing health.

10. SCHOOL PATTERN :   Adherence to school form after 25th
                             year: undeveloped dependency.

11. INDIVIDUAL LETTER FORMS: Originality and individuality.

3

Technique of Graphology

Simple   Definitions   of   Graphological   Terms:
CONNECTIONS : Strokes connecting the letters of a word.
DISCONNECTIONS: Omission of strokes connecting the letters of a
  word.
GARLAND : A gracious oval stroke as in a garland.
ANGULARITY : A stroke with a sharp angle.
ARCADES : An arched stroke resembling the architectural arcade.
THREADLIKE : An almost invisible connecting stroke, terminating in
  nothingness.

Connections

From the manner in which small letters are shaped and connected with each other we can recognize how the writer adapts himself to the environment and circumstances of his life. His capacity
for affection or his indifference, his inhibition or emotional expression, are mirrored in the connections of letters. Small letters usually
follow four patterns: garland, angular, arcade, and thread- or
spider-like. We also encounter all four connections mixed, revealing
the writer's versatility and easy adaptability to different circumstances in life. The genius and the highly developed intellectual

create an individual style of writing.

Very truly yours,

Connected Writing

A writing in which each word is written with one continuous stroke, each letter being joined to the succeeding one, is considered connected writing. This implies that the writer possesses reasoning powers and a logical mind.

Madam;
For some time I have

Mixed Connections

These mixed connections indicate adaptability to various circumstances. The writer is versatile; his interests are manifold. In this sample, "Madam" and "For" are disconnected, while the letters of the remaining words are perfectly joined.

hand

Disconnections

An interruption made in the connecting stroke by placing an i-dot or a t-bar crossing, is not considered disconnected writing. On the other hand, when the letters in a word are separated, i.e., without the connecting stroke, we find intuition and an ability to sense situations before they actually happen.

The intellectual writer with very quick tempo avoids futile strokes and often does not connect strokes. He displays simplicity in style and will not waste time or effort on any superfluous movement of the pen. The following is the constructive use of the disconnection of letters.

On the negative side, disconnected writing with narrow and arcade letters, often accompanied by a leftward slant, reveals the fact that the writer fears life and dares not face responsibilities. If the structure of the writing is dissolved, i.e., without form, rather than disconnected, it reveals acute negative qualities, such as mental imbalance or some mental disturbance, as in the following:

Small Letters

Small letters give the key to the writer's way of life and his subconscious thoughts. From them we can determine whether his life is harmonious or inharmonious, and can ascertain his disposition and temperament. In the small letters we also find the writer's personal motive, as expounded by Ludwig Klages.

Every nation has its standard unit for small letters. In general, the established size of the small letter for the school model is one-eighth of an inch, which is called medium size. If the writing is larger than the school model, it is called large writing; if smaller, it is called small, or very small.

Small

Medium

Large

The width of writing is measured by the proportion to the height of the letter. For instance, in the letter "n" we measure the distance between the two down strokes with the length of the down stroke itself. If the down stroke is longer than the distance between them, we have narrow writing; if shorter, it is considered wide writing.

In analyzing a handwriting, we must first take into consideration the size of the small letters, especially if the size is large as well as narrow. In cases of an uneven basic line, we often find that the size of letters is not uniform.

Garland

The garland connection, showing the gracious oval strokes of this diagram, generally shows a good-hearted nature, friendly and sociable. If the size is large, with uneven pressure and garland connections, fading out into the thread, it discloses the writer's instability of mind.

Angularity

Angularity, as illustrated in this diagram, is typical of self-contained and reserved characters who are prudent and discreet. They are neither pliable nor easily influenced. Angularity reveals good working qualities and a consistent personality. The writer may be obstinate, but he always displays persistence and reliability in the accomplishment of his tasks. Angularity is often a sign of manual and mechanical aptitude. The writer of angular letters is not the emotional type; he will rarely swerve from his principles. He is not impressionable, but a reasoner. We often find angularity in the handwritings of those of the leader type, who will pursue ideas and plans with energy and perseverance.

Arcade

If the arcade, or arched stroke of this diagram, appears in a narrow and compressed handwriting, we know that the writer is inhibited and may even be a neurotic. The arcade reveals lack of spontaneity and the writer places undue emphasis on the importance of conventionality. We also see the arcade connection in the handwriting of those who live in an environment of misunderstanding. The arcade is always a characteristic of some kind of artificiality.

On the other hand, the arcade, when it appears with unique shaping of letters, reveals a creative instinct; we find it in the handwritings of inventors, architects, and engineers, as well as in those of the genius. Arcades and angularity combined are present in the writings of mentally retarded children, because the natural connection should be the garland, which expresses something of the emotional life which is generally absent in the retarded.

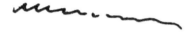

Thread or Spider-like

The thread or spider-like connection, the slurred and almost invisible connecting stroke which seems to evaporate at the end, is found in the irregularity of the small letters which form the basic line. This connection reflects the writer's nervous, impressionable, and emotional nature. He reacts quickly to various stimuli of the outer and inner world, and is mostly compliant, versatile, and subject to influences, either good or bad. He is impatient. His working habits are erratic, although often original and imaginative. The tempo in the threadlike connections is always quick, even hasty, showing that the writer may easily jump to conclusions. This style of writing is often used by the psychologist who comprehends the complicated and difficult shades of human character, and in the handwriting of a musician it is also a sign of the gift for improvisation.

The Personal Pronoun "I"

In the English language we must stress the importance of the capital "I" when it is used as the personal pronoun. English is the only language in which the personal pronoun of the first person singular is written with a capital. As is often brought out in the following chapters, the capital "I" as personal pronoun represents the writer's own idea of himself. It is his "ego." When simply written, it reflects modesty and a degree of refinement; exaggerated loops and artificial flourishes express ostentation and egotism. The following eleven samples reveal as many different facets of character.

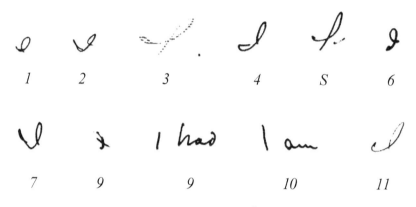

Personal Pronoun "I"

1) Small round, vertical: modesty, but self-assurance.
2) Small angular and closed: obstinate but modest.
3) Large, round, leaning: dependence on others, emotional.
4) Medium size, awkward: desire to be strong, but inhibited.
5) Medium size, uncertain, beginning with hook: needs encouragement.
6) Small, cramped: inferiority complex.
7) Angular with initial hook: egocentric and stubborn.
8) Leftward sling: inhibition.
9) and 10) Simplified: logic, independence, self-assured.
11) Medium size, leaning: dependence on others, needs encouragement.

Something About the Capitals

Capital letters tell us much of interest. Originality, talent, and mental capacity, as well as any deficiency or want of education, are disclosed by the formation of capitals. Many styles of capital letters are in use. The capital used by persons of education is plain, without ornamentation, although often eccentric and original in form. Em-

bellished capitals are generally used by those who have a fair amount of education mingled with a good deal of conceited ignorance and false pride. In such cases the capital letters are considerably adorned by loops, hooks, and curves, noticeable principally in the heads of the letters, or at their beginning. When the ego is over-inflated the capital letter is enlarged and ornamented with flourishes, in an obvious attempt to attract attention. The capital letter well-formed in size and shape is a genuine reflection of gentility and culture. The undersized capital indicates a lack of self-assurance and mistrust of one's ability. If the capital letter is of moderate size, with graceful formation, it is a constructive sign of the writer's well-rounded personality.

In the handwritings of those with creative minds, we encounter originality especially expressed in the capitals. In handwritings of the genius of the romantic period we see many ornate capitals which are an expression of this special style of writing. Ornate capitals must not be too harshly criticized when used by those from Latin countries, because their expression is more effusive than that of those from the Nordic countries. The Englishman's code of behavior, for example, is restrained; he therefore simplifies his capitals. When exaggerated capitals appear in the handwriting of an Englishman, we shall find, therefore, a parallel trait in his personality. The printed capital is modest and in good taste; it is modern and simple. We find it used in progressive groups. Librarians and filing clerks are required to use printed letters.

4.

Technique of Graphology

I-Dots and T-Bars

We believe that many graphologists attach too much importance to the marking of i-dots and t-bars. We should consider these marks merely as additions to the letter. There is a parallelism in the way the i-dots and t-bars are placed. If they are well-centered, we

conclude that the writer is punctual and exact; if they are placed high, it means idealism and optimism; if they are placed ahead of

the letter, impulsiveness; and if behind, procrastination. Discrepancies in the parallelism of i-dots and t-bars denote a conscious restraint or artificiality.

The crosses of the "t" are the index whereby to judge the temper of the writer. If those strokes are regular through the whole

page of writing, as in this sample, the writer possesses an even temper. If dashed off in quick, short strokes somewhat higher than the

letter itself, quick but short outbursts of anger may be expected; but if
the stroke is firm and black, great violence is obvious.

Uncertainty in character and temperament is shown by a variation in t-crossings. Sometimes the cross is firm and black, at other
times it is light, or omitted altogether, varying with each repetition of
the letter, like the opinions and sentiments of an undecided person.
The up and down strokes of the letter betray strength or weakness of
will.

Initial and Final Strokes
Hook Initial Stroke

The long stroke made at the beginning of a letter points to the
past; it shows an attachment to tradition, dependence upon the
customs of the home environment. As one matures, the initial stroke
should normally shorten or disappear, thus revealing that the individual has become independent and acquired self-reliance based on
his own mental and spiritual resources. The initial stroke symbolizes a
crutch on which to lean. The adult who writes with initial strokes
will never grow up, never live a full and successful life. The long

thin initial stroke shows resentment; the hook, acquisition.

know *and* *-(Hand*

1   2   3

when by The *in*

4   5

    The final stroke, or terminal: (1) if it sweeps gracefully, shows generosity, also a sense of humor and love of the beautiful; (2) flung down with a hook, it indicates aggressiveness and obstinacy; (3) long horizontal terminals indicate curiosity and sympathy for others, like a helping hand stretched out to the neighbor; (4) short terminals reveal abruptness and a tendency to be opinionated; (5) terminals rising upward show aspiration; curling back to self, they show egotism and self-love.

Shaping of Numbers

    Numbers are a symbol of the writer's attitude towards material values, an indication of how much importance the writer attaches to earthly possessions. We also see in the shaping of numbers the degree of the writer's flair for monetary matters.

Aug 14. 1941 *200 West 54th*

2   3

    The size of numbers (2), or the awkwardness of form (3), reveal the writer's inability to cope with financial questions in business and in private life. Number 2 displays more nimbleness in the shaping of numbers than in the writing of the text, revealing the writer's ability to reckon quickly and correctly. If the numbers are distinct, they disclose a capacity to handle monetary matters. Clear numbers are a sign of the writer's talent for mathematics and accounting, since great exactness and cleverness are displayed in the sure stroke and fluency with which the numbers are put on paper.

Study in Margins

Quite aside from handwriting characteristics, the placement of the writing on the page is a matter of significance. In letters, when the margin on both sides is in proportion to the width of paper and size of writing, we may conclude that the writer has a proper regard for neatness and order, accompanied by good taste, a sense of proportion, and balance and poise. If the margin is too narrow on both sides, or missing, it gives evidence of lack of proportion and good taste. If the margin is strongly crowded, it borders on confusion. When the margin on the left side is wide in proportion to the width of paper and size of writing, it proves the writer's wasteful attitude. The upper margin has relatively little significance. If it is extremely deep, it is almost always a sign of great respect to the addressee. This form of margin is most often used in conventional letters. In the case of a formal letter, the lower margin is of little significance; it will be kept neatly in proportion to the upper margin. More revealing is the lower margin in an informal letter. Some people want to go on indefinitely, but, half-ashamed to add another sheet, they "bubble over" into the side margin, after having crowded the lower margin to the very bottom. Such writers are friendly and impulsive, and enjoy social life.

Hampton–Marcuse Institute

200 West 54th Street

New York 19, N.Y.

Envelope

In considering margins it is also well to observe carefully the address on the envelope. Addresses, as in the attached sample, which do not deviate in form or size from the body of the writing will generally be found to confirm signs of proportion and good taste, culture, breeding, and artistic sense. They will be found to coincide with the indications shown by the margins in the body of the writing. Envelope addresses are very important; first, they carry several capital letters revealing important traits; and second, they express the writer's attitude toward public and social life.

The purpose of an address is that the letter should reach the addressee without difficulty. This purpose is served only by a high degree of legibility and clarity of writing and arrangement. Accordingly, many people do write more legibly on the envelope than in the letter itself.

Hampton - Marcuse Institute of Graph
200 West 54rd St.
New York 19, N. Y.

A case of illegibility on an envelope as above signifies the writer's psychological difficulty in observing the conventions. It indicates a special lack of adaptability which is characteristic of people who have difficulty in personal as well as in social contacts. Since an address is usually an expression of how the writer appears before the public, not an inner expression of his personality, we should never try to make an analysis from an address or signature alone, but always compare both with the whole body of the writing in order to gain a complete picture of the writer.

Signatures

The most personal part of a letter or document is, of course, the signature. But the signature alone, without any other writing, is not always a safe guide to character. Therefore, we must always be careful in the interpretation of any signature. In many instances the line

SIGNATURES

Iris Gordan

1

Sincerely yours,

W. A. Bower
Treasurer

2

Kenneth L. Jennings

3

4

Otto v. H. Whiteley

5

6

EDITOR

7

placed below or after a signature tells a great deal more than the way the actual name is written. The seven signatures reproduced herewith elaborate this quite clearly. (1) A curved, bending line below a signature, ending in a hook, indicates coquetry and love of effect. (2) An exaggerated, comma-like form of line means caprice, tempered by seriousness of thought and variety of ideas. (3) A person of unyielding will, fiery, yet determined, draws a firm hooked line after the signature. (4) Resolution is shown in a plain line. (5) Extreme caution, with full power to calculate effect and reason, is shown by straight dashes. (6) When a bar is placed below the signature or above, it means tenacity of purpose, in addition to extreme caution, and a dread of criticism and adverse opinions. (7) In this unusual signature the lines above are indicative of the author's incisive ability to discern trends and to protect his ideas in business.

Psychologically revealing are divergences in size between signatures and writing. In the case of a signature larger than the rest of the handwriting, the writer wants to overemphasize himself; perhaps a certain lack of self-reliance prompts him to be impressive. If the signature is smaller than the writing, we see self-consciousness and timidity expressed.

Spacing

Even spacing between words and lines, called vertical and horizontal spacing, reveals clarity of ideas, lucidity, and ability to separate thoughts, as in the following sample:

Dear Miss Marcuse :

Please send me

A well-spaced script gives evidence of the writer's culture, intelligence and perspicacity. In the way words and lines are arranged, a capacity for well-organized thinking is disclosed. A person capable of judging a situation objectively will employ a proper vertical and horizontal spacing in his script.

This sample exhibits a fairly even spacing. The distance between words and lines is not exactly the same, but there is an attempt to be clear and logical. We see lower loops entangled with the upper loops, disclosing some confusion in the emotional life.

The third sample shows complete lack of spacing; the letters are overcrowded, revealing the writer's confused and disorganized

mind. Too wide spacing in comparison with the size of the letters shows a tendency toward isolation and a difficulty in communicating

freely with others. If lower loops are overlong, reaching into the upper zone of the following line, it gives evidence of the writer's confused emotions in which unfulfilled love and sexual life are transposed to the realm of imagination.

5.

Discover What You Are

Before entering upon our discussion on analyzing your own handwriting, let us state one objection which is always mentioned in any discussion of analysis: "But I write differently all the time; even in the course of a page, my handwriting changes. How is it possible, then, that handwriting will give a reliable picture of my character and personality?"

Be prepared to answer this question somewhat as follows: If we omit changes of handwriting caused by such factors as a rusty pen, thick ink, rough paper or table surface, the principal cause of handwriting variation is psychological. Handwriting is mind-writing; the hand only holds the pen and obeys the command of the mind. Therefore, all our varying moods are unconsciously imprinted in the script, causing temporary changes. Since handwriting is closely related to personality, it must reflect these changes.

For your own information, you should know that every individual has personal preferences in style. Some people are conventional by nature, hence their handwriting will adhere to the copybook form. Others break away from convention and do things to suit themselves; their handwriting reflects these impulses and tendencies. The further the deviation from the school form, that is, from the generally used Palmer Method, the greater is the indication of individuality. If we omit the obvious factual evidence that people who write in a certain manner always behave in a certain way, and if the behavior pattern is exceptionally pronounced, the corresponding traits have a sound explanation.

From the beginning of time, man has tried in various ways to discover how the human mind works. After much research and investigation, a definite concept of the whole personality was discovered : that the individual's reasoning, his memory, his ingenuity, his judgment, and his ability determined his attitudes and interests. Observation of the whole personality in action was the next important step. Much of our behavior is based upon what our present need seems to be.

First of all, each of us must realize that there is a divine law governing the world and all mankind, expressing itself in the unchanging rhythm of the universe. When we perceive that there is such a rhythm, we begin to move with more freedom and better comprehend its source. Each human being has his own individual rhythm which is reflected in his handwriting, making it unique. When we become aware of this uniqueness in us, we are better able to direct our lives. Since every person is different, each must follow his individual expression of the rhythm operating within him. To understand this law it must be explored in terms of individual motivation and setting. However, before we follow the technical scheme and investigate details we must obtain a general impression of the whole picture, establishing the form level or quality.

Below Average

Average

Good

in the subject of graphology and I would

appreciate it if you would send me a

statement of your rates.

Superior

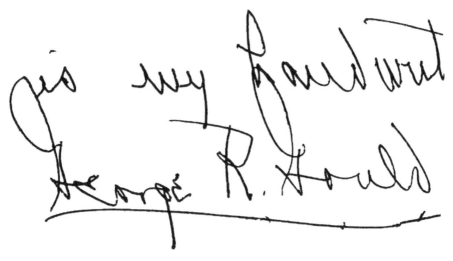

Scheme for Sample

Age:	fifty-eight
Sex:	male
Form Level:	average to good
Spacing:	even
Slant:	rightward
Basic Line:	even
Size:	medium
Initial Strokes:	present
Finals:	short, some abrupt
Regularity:	regular
Irregularity:	——————
Pressure	medium heavy

Dynamic:	fluent
Static:	——————
Rhythm:	good
I-dots:	high and ahead
T-bars:	long and heavy
Narrow:	medium
Wide:	——————
Connected:	connected
Disconnected:	——————
Numbers:	nimble
Margins:	proportioned
Zone:	middle

Resume

This fifty-eight-year-old man's handwriting reveals good intelligence through the good form level; the even spacing between lines and words shows that he uses his educational background in a clear and logical manner. The medium heavy, pasty pressure, garland connections, and rightward slant disclose his sanguine temperament and good-hearted nature; the even basic line reveals his mental and emotional stability.

Some of the formations of letters still adhere to the school model which, in addition to the initial strokes, shows that the writer has not escaped from the tradition of his home environment to complete independence of thought. The dynamic and rhythmic script, however, shows that he is not stubborn. On the contrary, he displays sufficient critical ability to admit his own shortcomings and to be aware of his strong traits. He is capable of judging himself and others objectively.

The regular and well-adjusted writing reveals his accuracy and dependability; he can be trusted absolutely. No change of slant hides any of his motives, the whole writing is fluent, going strictly to the right. The medium, almost slow tempo, discloses that he works slowly, almost fastidiously, but always intelligently. Since he still clings to the school pattern, we realize that he does not possess much initiative. However, the clear and well-spaced script shows that he makes the most of his assets, limiting himself to routine and habit. Nevertheless, he is a consistent worker, pursuing everything with concentration. The garland style reveals him as a good mixer, adaptable and sociable, although the abrupt and short finals show him to be selective in the choice of his friends.

The simple letters, even pressure, and firm stroke of the pen reveal his self-assured and poised personality: modest, friendly, and affectionate. The steadiness of the whole script testifies to his steadfast character; the high i-dots, his generally optimistic and idealistic outlook on life. Such a writer will be poised even in the face of adverse circumstances, and be willing and ready to assume responsibilities. His regard for the welfare and needs of others is disclosed in the warm pressure. Due to his sympathetic nature, he likes to be of help. The orderly script shows his practical sense which, in addition to his genuine love for people, makes him suited to social work as a counselor or personnel manager. The long and steady t-bars and comma-like i-dots reveal his sense of humor, good disposition, and enthusiasm. He will always be a pleasant associate and companion.

In the grapho-analytical procedure, a proper perception of rhythm, as well as of form level, depends largely on eye training and a good general sense of visual characteristics. Some basic rules can, of course, be given. In addition to the two guiding features, the form level and rhythm in handwriting, the general arrangement of the whole is essential to start your analysis on the way toward a closer investigation of graphic details, which in turn is indispensable.

Always bear in mind, however, that there are not many personalities sufficiently strong to depart from the conventional pattern of living. Most people feel secure only when they are following the prescribed pattern of their times. To break away from this pattern and become different, even to employ penmanship which departs from the orthodox, indicates originality, if not courage. Such originality definitely relates to the writer's degree of personality development, denoting at once the depth of his or her mental and emotional nature. This is reflected in the form level, or character, of your handwriting.

Your Sample as a Whole

Your sample of handwriting provides the frame for a proper interpretation of all graphic findings. One thing should be taken into consideration. However independent or individualistic you may be, you cannot escape being influenced by the life, habits and culture of your epoch. In the author's experience it is possible to make an objective rating of the form level of any script, after your eyes have been sharpened to discern the smallest variations.

After you have studied your handwriting in relation to the technique explained in the earlier chapters, read the following scheme and resume, and try to build up the analysis of your own handwriting in a similar way.

To know something of your temperament will facilitate making your analysis.

Temperament

The four temperaments are: choleric, melancholic, sanguine, and phlegmatic. The fourfold classification is useful because of certain fundamental dimensions of emotional response which it implies. Of all the writers on the subject, William Wundt, in *Grundzuege der Physiologischen Psychologies* seems most clearly to have perceived this fact. The four temperaments are essentially the resuiting combinations in a two-dimensional scale of emotionality, as in the following:

Choleric (Strong-Quick)

I am greatly . analysis work. and wish to you publish a book. useful purpose. I am a busy music I need some reference pertain hand writing.

Melancholic (Strong-Slow)

I have just finished u the interesting book on a graphology by Irene Mau

Sanguine (Weak-Quick)

I would appreciate it very much if you would send me

*some information in regards
the correspondence course in G.*

Phlegmatic (Weak-Slow)

*have just read
How To Analyze Handwriting
it very interesting and
if you still offered cours
If they are not too e,*

The following analyses will help you to see yourself more clearly and to do justice to your self-examination.

*some day I'll become
an artist. Who knows
what kind of an artist,
but an artist any way.*

This sample reveals a legible, well-spaced, and rhythmical script, although somewhat heedless. It is the expression of a gifted person who does not always exert sufficient effort to further his talent. It is the writing of a nineteen-year-old boy who, although endowed with a well-trained body and a good mind, does not seem to meet the demands for an independent artistic career for which he longs. The light and even pressure, with firmness of stroke, displays his good physique. Upper and lower zones are strongly emphasized; this discloses his artistic imagination and also that he can have his feet on the ground. The small letters denoting the middle zone, the practical and daily life, are not well-defined; they are also too small in comparison to the general size and are threadlike, revealing lack of mental decision. In the spontaneous and fluent script, in addition to the dashing t-bars, enthusiasm and artistic fire are disclosed. It is not an artificial writing; the flourishes are genuine, resulting from the writer's inner swing.

The case history begins when the mother of this boy asked a vocational counselor for advice. Training in photography was suggested and followed. After completing the training, the writer changed his mind and wanted to become a commercial artist. After examination of the light, fluent, rhythmic movement of this well-arranged writing, the mother was cautioned not to interfere with her son's desire. His talent for designing is forcefully expressed in the original display of flourishes, in addition to the good form level.

Although light pressure and thready writing point to flightiness and lack of persistence, there are many traits in this script which make up for this weakness, since the writer is still very young. The handwriting runs uninterruptedly to the right with great speed, disclosing the writer's definite purpose. In spite of the irregularity, the writing is legible. All these traits indicate that one can hopefully let him follow his inner vocation. He will not be lost in futile planning, but will ultimately work with a definite end in view.

My wife actually reads this draft. But then
22 years training   25 X 43

and thanks for your
good letter!

Alfred Einstein

My play for children is Androcles
& The Lion, it is also a play for adults.
Barries' Peter Pan, written throughout
down to supposed child-capacity, is in
that respect a failure. For children
there must always be passages of adult
depth or deeper.
A theatre for children should never
forget this. G. Bernard Shaw

The good form level, even spacing and heavy horizontal pressure, in this next sample reveal an efficient woman endowed with initiative, organizing talent, and business ability. The fluency of the writing, in addition to well-defined small letters, discloses qualities of quick decision and concentration. The emphasis in the lower zone betrays her materialistic attitude. She will appreciate only the value of money, be interested only in success from a financial point of view. The heavy and dashing t-bars bespeak her domineering nature. In comparison to the size of letters, the script is too narrow, revealing the fact that she associates with people only for her own ends, not out of sympathetic kindliness. The finals are pointed and descending with heavy pressure, illustrating her selfishness and lack of consideration for others. The capital letter "I," as personal pronoun in the second line, shows independence of thought and action. The energy expressed in these lines shows courage to start any new venture. This fifty-year-old woman will undoubtedly reach her goal. She will fight until she succeeds in achieving everything which she

has set out to accomplish.

some information about your course in Graphology. Thanking you very much and hoping to hear from

The average form level of this twenty-two-year-old girl's handwriting reveals average intelligence and common sense. The large and irregular script shows not only her enthusiasm in starting a new task, but also her impatience in pursuing it. The hasty tempo discloses lack of concentration and the fact that she is rather inclined to jump to conclusions. The over-long lower loops, which are interlinked with the other line, betray the girl's confused, unsatisfied sexual desire. The pressure is warm and even which, in addition to the garland connections and rightward slant, reveals an impressionable and warm-hearted nature. This young girl wants to be of help to others. She is kind, sympathetic, with a pronounced maternal instinct. It was recommended that she should make good use of her assets and, in addition, try to enlarge her interests by obtaining a broader general education. Her fondness for children could be utilized in a career as a kindergarten teacher or nurse.

Family Relationship in Handwriting

The following four samples belong to a family of parents and their two daughters, thirteen and fifteen years old. Before the younger daughter was born, the father became jealous of the great affection which had developed between his wife and the first daughter. Resemblance in temperament and appearance soon became evident and later there was a striking similarity in their handwriting. The girl began to treat the father as an outsider, an attitude which he deeply resented. Only at the birth of the younger daughter did the family happiness become established. The samples of the father and younger daughter show great similarity in writing, just as there is a remarkable resemblance between the child and the father in appearance and nature. The father gave this child all his

Father

The intermarr
blacks and whites
a people whose ski
The hair is strong
color of the skin is
yellow — In some c
Type is very attrac

Daughter (13 yrs.)

I really don't have anythi
to say but I would like to kno.
if you have the January "Life" n
there is an artical in it I wou
like to no what you have it and

Mother

each possesses; the characteristics each should encourage or guard agan and if you see sign of poor health will you please print that too? If I am asking

Daughter (15 yrs.)

swell. Its too cold for everybody down here, but I love it. It makes you want to do things; glad to be alive. How's Jerry, your mother and dad? Tell them I say hello. You haven't affection and was rewarded by her response. This family picture is a good example of how the infinite pattern of human beings can be woven into a beautiful design of living, and how handwriting reflects each personality, giving a clear picture of the character traits of each in relation to the others.

One of the most important results in the study of graphology is the deep insight the student often gains into his major faults and virtues. Traits that were hidden from him come to light in a constructive manner. He becomes his own critic, and quietly goes about correcting his faults to his own satisfaction, and to that of all who come in contact with him.

Dear Mrs. Marcusse :

Enclosed please find $5.00 me
as full payment for your course in
About your recent analysis
handwriting. I am white, male, ri
28 yrs. old. In general I think
some very good interpetations and

Here is an interesting case in point, exemplifying the very thing we have just stated. Both of the scripts were written by the same man two years apart. A most remarkable change is evident in them. The second sample shows an improvement even to anyone without the slightest knowledge of graphology. To be specific, we shall show the changes as they appear. Citing the traits in the first script, we see many pointed consonants (narrow-mindedness), and underslung endings, (selfishness), and an involved capital "E" (provincialism). The downward slanted t-bars point to the lower zone (sarcasm with the intent to hurt). The personal pronoun "I" squeezes itself into the middle zone (undeveloped ego), with uncertainty of strokes and negative disconnections (absolutely no insight into himself or others). Most conspicuous is the narrowness of the whole script. This last reveals the fear and inhibition of narrow vision.

Dear Ladies:

this is just a note to l

that I haven't given up

might appear so.   E.C.S

Like a curtain drawn back from a window, we see in the second sample the same man two years later. Here he is in his true light, showing his success in overcoming the traits which were not a true part of his make-up. Note the beautiful, graceful capital "E" as contrasted to this same letter in the first sample. A straightforward generosity, insight, and freedom of thought and action, as well as expression in speech, have so changed this script that it is now a privilege to know this young man, as he knows himself.

Here is the perfect example of a student of graphology who used his knowledge as a means for becoming objective, instead of subjective. He is now a positive extrovert instead of a negative introvert.

E.Sherarty Jr.

6.

Handwriting of the Child

Each child is a personality peculiar to himself. Each must be considered separately and given his own chance. The drive for satisfaction is stronger in some children than in others. Some take denials in a cringing manner, some more pugnaciously. Some children withdraw, others revolt. Some retire into themselves; they build a more or less impermeable wall around themselves. Others make attempts to attack. Some move away from the scene; others move aggressively into it.

The child who assumes a pugnacious attitude to protect himself against hurt and frustration is the child whom grown-ups are apt to call "bad." The child who withdraws is less likely to be noticed; he passes often as "good." The fact that he makes much less trouble for those about him, inclines his elders in turn to consider his problems less serious than those of his pugnacious brother. However, his problems, instead of being less serious, are in reality much greater. He is more greatly in need of help. He is more liable to grow into the kind of person who "breaks" or develops mental illness.

It is true that children sometimes manage to find for their pressures outlets which are socially acceptable. The boy who becomes a fearless rider or a champion marksman may have developed these

69

activities as a means of getting even with a dominating father by displaying his own strength. Symbolically, he conquers his father as he conquers a horse or target. The girl who becomes a successful costume designer may be the very girl who was self-conscious about her own body, and so projects a hidden desire to display herself onto those for whom she designs clothes. However, the fact remains that even though these people are successful, they are using energy to keep down the very same emotional pain which drives them on. The energy which they drain in this manner, if utilized for accomplishment, could make it possible for them to attain their objective with less strain and tension. Accomplishment would be more integrated in their endeavors, and they would not be dissipating their energies wastefully.

When problems are present in children, they must be seen in the context of the child's whole life. His entire environment will be important. When he is young, his parents will be the central part of that environment. Their frustrations and their satisfactions will influence him and will have a definite effect on his personality. It is obvious that the best time to eliminate wrong conceptions of life is in childhood. It is far easier to do it then, than at a later period in life.

What kind of children do parents want? How many have clearly formulated and set down a description of the personality they would like for their son or daughter? Thinking about the objective of child training is complicated by a certain inconsistency in social values. What is a "well-disciplined child?" Most people will readily agree that a well-disciplined child should respond to the wishes of adults, to demands outside himself. Most important, however, is that orders should be given, not to accommodate adults, but for the child's own well-being. A child wishes to obey because he feels inadequate to cope with life. However, he will feel secure only if convinced that love, understanding, and dependability guide his parents.

Although analyzing a child's handwriting needs some deviations from analyzing those of the adult, we can apply the same rules, with the exception of irregularity and steadiness of strokes. When the child acquires some degree of skill, the speed increases and regularity begins to improve. The degree of deviation from the school pattern has the same significance as in handwritings of the adult. By studying the scripts of several children of the same age and class, as presented in this chapter, we gain good information of the child's co-ordination, emotional balance, mental growth, and acquisition of the language. The following analyses are all of children eleven years old. The findings have been confirmed by their teacher.

Theresa's script discloses average intelligence in the average form level. Large-size letters, medium light pressure, and slow tempo show an easy-going nature and a tendency toward laziness. Some of the capitals are embellished, revealing some vanity for good grades, but the continual change of slant betrays her lack of concentration and ambition, and the necessary effort to work harder in order to obtain them. She certainly will not be one of the best in her class. Some fat lower loops reveal this little girl's inclination to eat more than she needs, especially sweets, which will increase her weight, making her still lazier. This girl lacks drive, both in mental and physical activities. She always needs to be spurred and admonished to do her tasks.

Are you feeling o.K. ? Ho you? Well you be ha How soon will you be Very soon ? your class ma

Stephen.

At first sight it is obvious that Stephen is a stutterer. Sudden hesitation between letters and rewriting reveal this fact. This boy is highly emotional: those about him are incapable of coping with such an emotional disturbance as his. Although the letters display some genuine intelligence, his mental development is below average and he cannot work consistently for any length of time. With great effort he may succeed for a short period in concentrating on his tasks, but is not quite up to competing with normal children of his age. His actions and reactions are very slow; he also lacks co-ordination. With psychological guidance this boy could be helped to progress, although he would advance slowly. This boy might develop such an inferiority complex that he would feel incompetent to meet social demands made upon him and become an outsider before he grows into adolescence. The emotional disturbance which caused his handicap should be treated now.

Kenneth's script is surprising in its good arrangement and even

I'm very sorry we w—... ... weeks were doing nice things during this time. ...ad or for Scholastics ... today ... you must be ... you must it.

Truly You

Kenneth

spacing. This shows that the boy has already developed a clear and logical mind. The high-climbing letters reveal aspiration and ambition to be the best in the class. There is good speed in these lines, but also hastiness, which shows his good mind and alertness on the one hand, and on the other impatience and flightiness. The boy wants to be better than his classmates, and he resorts to all sorts of tricks to reach his goal. He is something of a schemer and he might not always be trusted to speak the truth. These facts are revealed by concealing strokes; in the letter "t" the downstroke is covered with the up stroke. His physical make-up is delicate and lags behind his mental development. The pressure is light and uneven. The narrowness and abrupt endings reveal that he resents his physical inadequacy and is jealous of other children who are stronger. This makes him inhibited in spite of his mental superiority.

Donald's handwriting displays an inferior form level revealing that his intelligence is below average. The unfirm strokes, uneven pressure, and continual change of slant disclose a poor co-ordination caused by insufficient mental adjustment. We notice the personal pronoun 'I' is written with more certainty than the other letters,

analyze my handwriting.
I wonder if you can tell me if
successful in my coming test
A I would be very nice
why don't you come out to
Hope to see you soon.

Your nephew

Donald.

which shows his desire for physical and mental expression. However, since he has difficulty in following what the teacher says and keeping his thoughts on the subject, he feels incompetent. The extreme irregularity discloses his lack of understanding for any systematic work. He is jumpy, and starts his tasks, but works sporadically, doing different subjects at the same time without bringing anything to a definite conclusion. The very slowness of this script seems to reveal a lazy and slow boy; but, in fact, it is lack of understanding rather than laziness. Some heavy pressure at t-bars reveals rebellion, and the writing as a whole presents a picture of an unhappy child. Since Donald must be considered as a backward child, it will be advisable to transfer him to a class for retarded children until he gains the capacity to cope with the demands of classmates. He is neither emotionally nor mentally ready to compete with children of his age at this time. Here again we have an example of a child whose unfortunate home environment shows in his handwriting. The uncertainty of strokes, in addition to heavy pressure on t-bars, reveals incompetence and rebellion. If the parents will not accept the advice to place the boy in a special school, it is possible that he may become a juvenile delinquent.

I hope you get well soon. I n
we are haveing a poster contest. You
missed a lot of work. We won the
membership. Somebody paid for.
We won a nice prize. I no you
like it.

Your Friend
Ronnie

Ronnie's handwriting shows an intelligence above average, and good reasoning powers in the good form level and even spacing between words. The firm strokes, even pressure, and emphasized upper zone disclose his ambition and aspiration to be the best in the class. His retentive memory is shown in the well-defined small letters. The personal pronoun "I" is remarkably developed in its simplification, revealing self-assurance and his aspiration to recite and speak before the class. The narrowness and short finals disclose that he will not be quite as successful in his personal relationship with classmates. This boy has some difficulty in establishing friendly relations with children of his own age. Although he wants to be with children, he lacks the ability to contact them socially. He also is not prepared to share, either his knowledge or mere material possessions. The stroke is somewhat wiry, which shows that Ronnie is obstinate, never pliable. He has built up in his mind the idea that he knows best and will not accept a different opinion.

Dear Madam :—

I am a boy eleven years of age. U please analyze my handwriting ? I he will please try to find something nice to sa cause my mother thinks I am very naugh

"2 7 "

This boy has learned to form his letters with skill and certainty; the spacing between words and lines is fairly even. These graphic traits show that the boy has a capacity for clear reasoning, in addition to a strong will, bordering on obstinacy. This little boy wants his own way and, if crossed, displays great temper. The t-bars are very heavy in contrast to the light, pasty pressure. The good form level discloses his good intelligence, and he should be allowed to develop independently, but under wise supervision, because interference may aggravate his high-strung nature. The "I," as personal pronoun, shows more individuality and freedom than the rest of the writing, which discloses that he is badly in need of a means of self-expression. The "I" in the last line is especially interesting; it is much smaller. Here he identifies himself with what he writes and becomes very humble.

Janie displays an exceptionally well-organized mind and independence of thought in this well-spaced and regular script of high form level. The garland connections and light and even pressure reveal her gentle and affectionate nature and even disposition.

I brought my crayons school today. Did you bring yours in yet?

I'm glad your mother wanted to join the P. T. We are getting a magnetic board for the prize. It will be in the class tomorrow.

Your best friend,

Janie

While the high-climbing upper loops disclose her imagination, the narrow letters and light pressure show a rather sensitive nature which easily takes offense. Her vital imagination will magnify any affront out of all proportion. This fact is corroborated by the open stems of the letter "t." The little girl is not demonstrative, but will suffer inwardly. Since she is so well-disciplined, she tries to conceal her hurt feelings. There is a tendency to shrink when approached, instead of fighting back or voicing her protests. She is timid (narrowness), and suffers if neglected or even reprimanded. The high degree of rightward slant reveals her highly emotional nature. The whole writing gives the impression that this child is in need of affection and understanding. Loving guidance would bring her out of her shell. There is a fine personality hidden in this rather shy girl, expressed in this script. Encouragement will benefit her, and neither teacher nor parents should spare appreciation, because she is very modest and self-critical.

Fred's low form level in writing this sample shows that his I.Q. is not very high. This puts him at a disadvantage at the start. The difficulty may be partly traced to a foreign influence in the home, which slowed his understanding of phonetics in English. Consequently he makes mistakes in spelling. While he is not the brightest pupil in the class, he can keep up with his mates. This boy desires to do his work better, and this carries him along, even if he is slow in grasping what the teacher has to say. He certainly needs help. The ink-filled, tightly closed and rolled-in letters reveal his inhibition in expressing himself. He is awkward, and feels inferior toward the other children. This makes him timid and uncertain to such an extent that he forgets what he means to say. The heavy pressure, especially in the t-bars, shows physical development and determination to excel in sports. However, the lack of co-ordination will keep him back even in this activity. It seems safe to say that the boy would be better off in a boarding school, away from his home influence, where he could have intelligent guidance.

Teddy's good form level and even spacing reveal a bright child; one who grasps quickly and knows how to express clearly what he

We won first prize for getting our P.T.A. money in. We didn't get our prize yet. I hope you are well soon. Our p t a, puppy will be a magnetic bulletin board

Your classmate

Teddy

wishes to say. The fluency of the writing without any change of slant indicates that the boy is developed mentally and physically beyond his age. The equal size of letters shows that he has already gained a clear understanding of his subjects in school. The garland style, in addition to the good length of the terminals, reveals his favorable disposition; he is affectionate and kind, and will always be ready to help other children. That he is imaginative and possesses individual and original ideas is seen in the emphasis on the upper zone. The medium, pasty pressure gives us the clue to his mental and physical soundness. Certainly he is affable and will attract friends easily.

Arthur is a boy of good intelligence, and a clear and logical thinker. He seems far advanced intellectually for his eleven years. This is brought out in the individual formation of letters and general appearance, or form level. Artistic in temperament, he fears to express himself before other children. This feeling of inferiority is due to his difference in temperament rather than in ability. He tries to put on a front of braggadocio. The cartoon method of drawing is one way of ingratiating himself with the others. The smallness of letters reveals his observant, meditative nature. He needs more en-

I miss you very much. He's a joke slip I think you'd like.

Joe and Bob in the dentist
Joe those
teeth of yours a
buitiful
they are?
yeah but t
gums have to c
out!

Yours truly
Arthur

couragement than is apparent. The heavy, pasty, pressure shows a rather impressionable child without too much firmness and decision. He is very sensitive (open "t" stems) and easily hurt. He may be easily imposed upon.

The sense of light and shade in the warm pressure of Sandra's handwriting is the key to her color sense and musical talent. Temperamental by nature, her gaiety can suddenly change to tears and sadness, which is expressed in the continual change of slant. On the other hand, she can quickly be taken out of her unhappiness. There is a shallow garland style and full lower loops, which explain her *board. She also put the time we are to do it on the black-board. You'd put $1.00 in the S. L. T., you and we ____. We will get a ____ with ballet ____. x.*

you ____ ____, in ____

quick affectionate nature. Her feelings may not be too lasting or deep, but she will co-operate with her classmates. Being tactful and discreet enough to keep a secret (closed "a's" and "o's"), she has already gained the ability to take care of her own interests (very short terminals). Of a sanguine and phlegmatic temperament, she is obedient and will follow directions. There is a strong desire and aptitude in this girl for physical expression as, for instance, dancing. Yet, lacking in ambition, she needs urging and prodding to do anything systematically.

7.

Adolescent Handwriting

The adult who has had a thoroughly satisfying infancy and childhood can more easily withstand later frustrations. No single reversal, either financial or emotional, ever causes a mental breakdown. When an adult gives way in the face of misfortunes, it is only because he still carries with him the unhealed emotional scars of an earlier period. The event which seemingly causes the breakdown serves merely to reopen and irritate the wound.

Clinical psychologists and others dealing with adolescents who

This rebellious, maladjusted youth asked professional advice on his condition in his first letter. Two years later his second letter clearly shows that he acted on it.

lie, steal, or play truant have often remarked that there are few real problem adolescents, but a great many problem parents. This means that unresolved emotional conflicts in the parents are often the root of the problem behavior exhibited by the adolescent. There has been a growing conviction that the best parents and teachers are not necessarily those who know the most about the physical, mental, and emotional growth of children, but those who are themselves well-adjusted and well-integrated. Children learn by example.

It is incorrect to believe that children are maladjusted because they inherit the mental instability of their parents. Unstable parents jeopardize the normal development of their children. Self-knowledge and self-adjustment are basic essentials in parents and teachers if they are to discharge their obligations satisfactorily. The positive aim of child guidance should be the development of a well-integrated personality exhibiting the characteristics of good mental health which we describe in the chapter on mental disease. It is of paramount importance that parents and teachers remind themselves constantly of the aims which we explained in our description of mental health, and consider whether their methods of guidance are likely to achieve the goal.

Since sex crimes among adolescents are so frequent, we observe that almost all criminal tendencies in teenagers are traceable to some form of misconception about sex. It is of the greatest importance that adolescents have the best example at home, where love and understanding will guide them on the right road of life. If adults treat sex exactly as they treat any other topic, giving the adolescent answers to all his questions and just as much information as he can understand, sexual curiosity will subside because it is satisfied. Therefore, the best way to prevent young people from being obsessed with sex is to explain just as much about it as they care to know.

These two samples are the scripts of parents who did not agree about how to bring up their twelve-year-old daughter, whose handwriting is illustrated in the third sample. The mother is a woman of thirty-three. The average form level and fairly even spacing be-

Dear Mrs. Marcuse —
I have read with into
your daily column and
would greatly appreciat
having my handwriting
analyzed — I am thirty
three years old, femal

tween words and lines reveal average intelligence and education.
The angular connections, in addition to the triangular lower loops,
betray her obstinacy and consistency. The personal pronoun "I" is
higher than other capitals, showing the writer's high opinion of herself. The first letter in the salutation "D" is involved, as well as all
the vowels, disclosing this woman's self-centered and narrow mind.
She is not open to any suggestion, but will have her own way at all
costs. She is convinced that she knows everything better and will
violently assert herself. This is revealed by the sudden pressure on
horizontal strokes. The long initial strokes with the hook confirm
these statements; the writer is selfish, immature, and undeveloped
as a personality.

The father is a man of thirty-three. The form level is higher
than that of the wife, revealing the man's good intelligence and education. The personal pronoun "I" at the beginning shows this man's
vanity and feeling of importance. This fact is corroborated by some

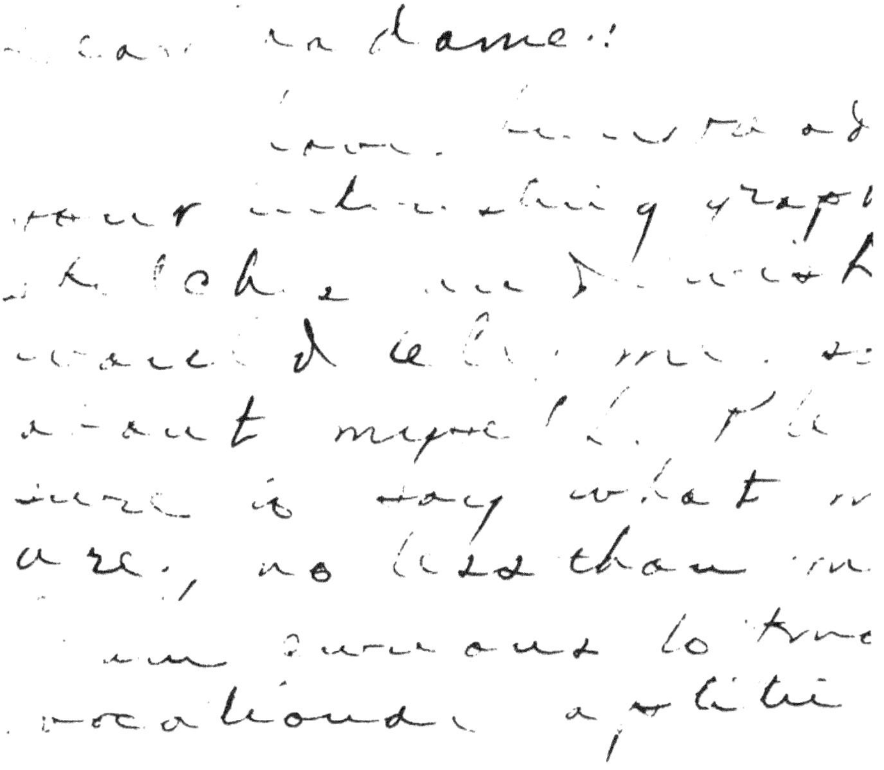

futile flourishes. The garlands are shallow, running out into a thread; this betrays his superficial and easy-going nature. The fluency and speed show that he is a man who knows how to get around and make a success of his career. He is enthusiastic, somewhat of a dreamer. Since he dreamed all his life of being an actor, but felt that his ambition had been frustrated, he had transferred his hopes to his little daughter, urging her to take advantage of the opportunity denied him. It is understandable that the mother opposed his plans. Lacking in any understanding for such a career, she foresaw only unhappiness for their child.

The daughter's writing shows good intelligence in the individual formation of letters and the even spacing between words. The heavy t-bars reflect her will power. However, the continual change in slant, together with the light and uneven pressure, reveals her

It is twice blessed; It l
_that gives and him tha
mightiest in the mightie
the throne'd monarch bet
crown ;
His scepter shows the fo
power, the attribute to a

emotional instability and the fact that she is torn between two forces. Because of her parents' continual disagreement over her, she has not found that inner harmony which is conducive to a normal and gradual development. The suggestion to the parents was to abandon their own desires and ambitions in the interest of the child's well-being and to wait for her to mature and make her own decisions.

The three following samples present another example of family disagreement and its effect upon the child.

This is the handwriting of a thirty-nine-year-old man, husband

Please describe my cha
also what will my prosp
in the near future.
Enclosed you will find 2
Postage stamps.
Thanks

to the writer of the next sample. The very regular, well spaced script, with an average form level, reveals a reliable and loyal man of practical intelligence and good common sense. The light pressure and high degree of rightward slant show his mild and affectionate nature, but also a relatively weak personality. The simple letters, in addition to the steady basic line, reveal his steady emotions and capacity to manage his life and career successfully. The thin and long t-bars disclose some enthusiasm, but the extreme regularity shows that everything will be well under control. The garlands betray his affectionate feelings.

The handwriting of the wife displays many hooks and leftward slings, in addition to sharp angular connections, revealing a deceptive nature which is intolerant and quarrelsome. The futile adornments show her vanity, and the tightly closed ovals her selfishness. The continual change of slant, hasty tempo, and light and uneven pressure disclose an emotionally disturbed person who, unhappy herself, cannot bring out any harmony or happiness around her. Since the form level reveals only average intelligence and the personal pronoun 'T' her feeling of importance, she will overrate herself. This, in addition to her instability, will always create disturbance around her wherever she goes, and especially in her home. Always quarrelsome, she becomes aggressive at times.

The son's script greatly resembles his father's. Independence of letters reveals his intelligence, and the regularity, consistency in accomplishing his school work. The boy is twelve years old and has acquired considerable independence of thought and action for his age. Here we also see the light pressure, but it is uneven and there are falling endings. This child possesses his father's sensitivity, as well as his tender disposition. The pressure betrays his supersensitive nature and delicate health. Since there was no doubt that the mother has a disturbing influence on both the father and the child, it was recommended that the child be sent to a boarding school, thus leaving the parents to work out their own problems.

The next sample is the script of an epileptic boy of seventeen. We see arrested development in the inferior form level and also in the uncertain strokes. The pressure is uneven and at some places it is cramped and does not flow. A magnifying glass will show this fact very clearly. However, the personal pronoun "I" at the beginning of each line reveals that he has self-confidence because it is written with more freedom and certainty. Some angularity reveals mechanical aptitude; mostly the connections are arcade, indicating his han-

I am a boy of 17 teen

I got a Tefforted of man

I too to take pictures

dicap. This mechanical aptitude was pointed out to him and he learned a trade. Although he could not regularly attend classes, he learned enough to be able to work at home and earn some money.

that I could I'm so glad that write you th I'm on my way to a (better, brighter and I realth is outlo on life.

Here we have the script of a sixteen-year-old girl, displaying pasty pressure in an irregular movement, in addition to even spacing between words. These graphic traits disclose an impressionable person, who is intelligent, clear, and logical of mind. The irregularity betrays this girl's emotionally unstable condition; but that this is a temporary state of mind is disclosed in a fairly even basic line coupled with unchanging and rightward slant. Although, when this sample was written, the girl was very upset because of the pending divorce proceedings of her parents, the personal pronoun 'I' shows courage in its steadiness. The good form level reveals this girl's intelligence and an emotional maturity advanced far beyond that of other children of her age.

*from High School I do not belong
clubs, but I do attend dances, an
Thanking you very much and hope
very soon.*

The writer of this sample is a girl of seventeen. The good form level, even spacing, medium heavy and even pressure all disclose an intelligent person who has gained independence of thought and is clear and logical. She is consistent in her working habits and has a definite purpose in life. The personal pronoun "I" is larger than the other letters, but closed up; this shows her self-assurance on the one hand, and on the other, little insight into others. The leftward slant reveals reserve which, in addition to the tightly closed ovals betrays this girl's self-contained, somewhat secretive nature. She hides her real feelings. The full lower loops, which are at times broken back, disclose the girl's overemphasis in her imagination on the importance of sex. This young girl has the capacity of becoming an efficient person in whatever career she will choose. However, she needs some help in clarifying her confused timidity toward the opposite sex and her affinity for her own. This would give her a normal understanding of herself and better relationships with others.

In our next example, the good form level and even spacing between words in the handwriting of this fifteen-year-old girl reveals good intelligence, originality, and a clear and logical mind. The omissions of initial strokes shows that she has achieved independence of thought and action far beyond her age. However, the personal pronoun "I" leans somewhat on its back, which discloses that the girl still needs guidance; the high degree of rightward slant corroborates this fact, betraying her willingness to submit to good counsel. The writer knows how to organize and systematize her tasks;

there is regularity and good adjustment in the whole script. Her

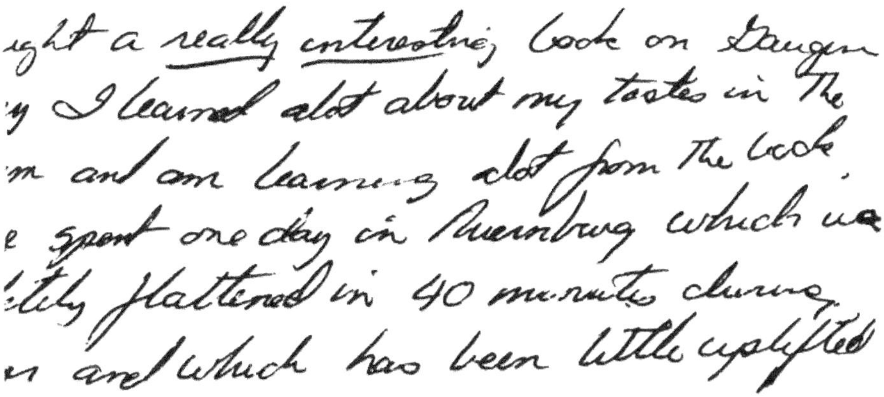
ight a really interesting book on Daugen
y I learned alot about my tastes in The
m and am learning alot from the book.
e spent one day in Nuernburg which wa
etely flattened in 40 minutes during
s and which has been little uplifted

good taste and appreciation for good literature are apparent in the fluency with which the letters "g" and "f" are written. The pasty pressure and steadiness of the writing movement show that this young girl has inner strength and is extremely impressionable. From the harmonious arrangement of the whole script we gather the idea that the author of these lines is enjoying a peaceful and affectionate home environment. The consistent slant discloses her emotional security, as well as her sensitive impression of art and beautiful objects.

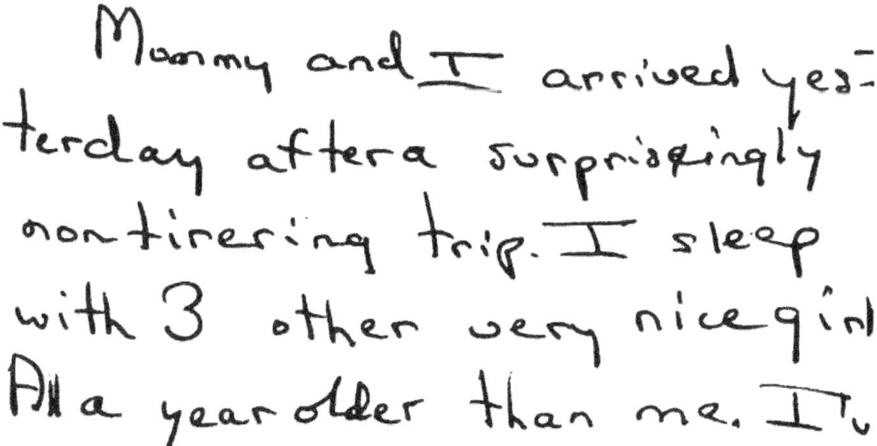
Mommy and I arrived yes-
terday after a surprisingly
non tiresing trip. I sleep
with 3 other very nice girl
All a year older than me. I'v
discovered that I lve h...

One would hardly believe that the writer of this sample is a girl

of thirteen. The high form level and even spacing testify to a surprisingly mature and original personality. The well-proportioned and
mostly vertical script shows that she is organized and reserved, on
the one hand and, on the other, lively and impulsive as expressed in
the rapid tempo and some change of slant. The personal pronoun
"I" discloses a high degree of inner stability. The warm and heavy
pressure is dynamic, showing perspective. This reveals the girl's
musical talent and very artistic personality. One can perceive that
this little girl has every promise of developing into an important person, blessed with many talents.

The writer of the following sample is an eighteen-year-old boy
who is a drug addict and juvenile delinquent. The smeary pressure
and uneven basic line show his addiction and emotional disturbance.
The handwriting displays a form level below average; letters are undefined and illegible. However, the spacing is fairly even and some
letters show some individuality, betraying the boy's natural intelligence. The connections within the words are mostly angular, running
out into a thread. Some angular lower loops, with heavy pressure on
t-bars, reveal his rebellion. The boy was an unhappy child who tried
often to overcome his handicaps, but failed because he could not
control his impulses. The case history reveals that he was a stutterer
in childhood and could not compete with children of his class
because of slowness of perception. His parents, of good finan-

cial standing, spoiled and pampered him on the one hand, and on the other showed the utmost incompetence in handling this problem. They did not accept professional advice, but were unhappy, almost ashamed, that their only child was so different from other children. At the age of sixteen the boy ran away from home. He joined a gang and became a drug addict and juvenile delinquent. He was soon placed in a reformatory by the authorities. This is a perfect example of how important it is to give help in early childhood, before the child grows into adolescence. This tragedy could have been avoided if the parents had been open to advice, instead of embarrassed over their failure to help him themselves.

8.

As Vocational Guidance

All human beings constantly strive to achieve some definite goal. Many are not aware of what they seek; others have a definite aim. If we really understood ourselves, we would see that every single desire is directed toward fulfilling a discernible need. Too often we feel that our own problem is unique. We hesitate to admit the sort of thing we most desire. We can be helped, however, by realizing that many of our innermost wants are universal.

In striving toward our goal, we must feel secure within ourselves and certain of our aims. Without this, we can have no peace. Inward peace results from spiritual strength. Affection and response from others aid in giving us a sense of well-being. Feeling that we have a place in the world—that we belong—helps in the building of security. The competitive nature of our society puts great emphasis on achievement. The man who is successful is the man who achieves most in his endeavors. Not everyone can excel in his efforts, but everyone can utilize his talents to their greatest extent.

Utilization of Talents

Talent and aptitude are in themselves not sufficient for a successful career; such other qualities as will make of personality an integrated whole are equally vital. These attributes include alertness, temperament, emotional or sensory quality, and the will to accomplish. Alertness is necessary in order to gain a proper aspect of life and to regulate one's reactions. Temperament is a part of the emotional life, representing the deepest incentives to both thought and action. (See "Temperament," in *Applied Graphology,* by Irene Marcuse.) Feeling is the ordinary stimulus to action; emotion is a violent form of feeling. Our will drives our motive power and inherent energy; it is the free expression of our fundamental urge to act. Since the will is usually considered highly significant, one speaks of those with strong wills as those whose lives are motivated by a desire to dominate others. They usually become leaders.

No one is born without some inherent talent. It is important to realize this fact, for it gives each of us self-esteem, whereas the feeling of being totally without a special talent leads to self-deprecation. Life's demand upon each one of us is for activity, not idleness; for self-discovery, not self-deprecation. Handwriting analysis will uncover our individual talent, and show us how to utilize it. The purpose of graphological analyses is to make known the man within. Thus we contribute to the betterment of human relations. Graphology also develops insight into oneself and others. By knowing the emotions and problems of others, we can employ more tolerance, avoid antagonizing explosive natures, and create unity and happiness.

J'accuse,

eighteen years old. Please tell me

you think that I shall succeed.

that I am planning on entering so

? me if I have any artistic ability.

Our first case involves the handwriting of a girl of eighteen. The small, simplified letters reveal her faculty for concentration and sustained effort and her will to succeed. The good form level shows individuality, intelligence, and independence of thought. Her emotional development has lagged far behind her mental maturity. The capital letter "I" as personal pronoun reveals timidity and self-consciousness; this letter is not freely written, but is cramped and involved. The uneven basic line discloses emotional instability and lack of self-assurance. All these characteristics point to the fact that the writer will for the present not be successful in dealing with people. After she has had further development and training, she may become a writer because she possesses intellectual qualities. She is a "reasoning" rather than a "feeling" type, as shown by her well-defined and clear letters. She should concentrate her efforts on writing factual rather than imaginative subjects until she develops more imaginative strength. The regularity of this script shows her good qualities of workmanship. The heavy t-bars in this light-pressure writing discloses some temper. The firmness of letters shows that this young girl is ambitious to have a career and to become

The next sample is the script of a young woman of twenty-two. She is endowed with average, practical intelligence, as revealed by letters which conform to the school model. In choosing to become a typist she shows that she understands her vocational aptitude. The leftward slant reveals reserve, and the broken-back lower loops, in addition to the arcade connections, reveal her inhibited nature. The firm pressure and even spacing between words disclose the writer's ability to apply herself and the will power to do consistently good work. Her emotional life is somewhat frustrated and immature, as can be seen in the leftward slings of the lower loops. Her temperament is actually sanguine, but through frustration she has developed in the opposite direction, as an introvert, and is timid and shy. Since she is an introvert and distrustful of people, she needs to be awakened to a more co-operative attitude toward, and love for, her fellow beings if she is to acquire the confidence of her co-workers.

my dear Madame Marcuse:
I should be grateful
for your analysis of my
potentialities, and —

Our third case involves a young woman of twenty-two, who is more original than the last writer. Her individual letter formations reveal her intelligence and her talent for commercial art work. In spite of her sense of humor, which is disclosed in the wavy t-bars, her disposition is an unfortunate one. Her changing moods and emotional instability are shown by the continual change of slant and in the uneven basic line. Because of her variable moods, she is not pleasant to associate or work with, for she displays uncontrolled temper. Although she is intelligent and capable of doing good work, she is not stable enough to concentrate. She must discipline herself until she has learned to accomplish a given task. She is enthusiastic in starting any new work, but her enthusiasm subsides as soon as she does not see immediate results. Because she is impulsive and impatient, she soon tires and loses interest in a project. While it is important to have talent, this writer finds it impossible to focus her abilities on any given medium.

The next sample is that of a man of forty. It is an original script; this well-developed upper zone reveals creative imagination in commercial art. Letter forms show independence of thought and action. The spacing between words and lines is even, disclosing that the writer will go his own individual way to attain success in his career, since he is endowed with both talent and the power of application. Although a humanitarian spirit is pictured in the large tri-

Dear Miss Siren

I would like tell me something my handwriting.

angular lower loop of the letter "y" in the first word of the third line, this is contradicted by the extremely wide spacing between words, which shows that this man is not too communicative. He prefers to be an onlooker and enjoys his own company more than the society of others. He is supercilious and feels superior to other people. The handwriting runs fluently to the right, without interruption and with good speed, disclosing this man's logical mind, quick perception, and steadiness of purpose.

The writer of the next specimen is a young man of twenty-one. The involved leftward lower loops reveal a person who is greatly absorbed in himself and has not yet attained freedom in establishing his individuality. The above-average form level betrays some originality, but the flourished script displays vanity and conceit. The aforementioned lower loops, involved and turned back on themselves, reveal his selfish nature. He is self-centered and has a narrow outlook on life. This young man possesses creative imagination but, since he is untrained, he has not found the right medium for express-

Dear Irene Marcuse

I would like you to tell

something about my handwriting

ing himself. The even spacing between words shows that he is capable of attending to his work, but the light pressure indicates that he needs to develop inner moral strength. The threadlike connections reveal that he is easily distracted and has not yet reached the point where he can put his imagination to practical use. So far, he seems to be content to waste his time and ability in daydreaming.

Dear Irene Marcuse

I should appreciate your telling m

handwriting

June.30 1949

The handwriting of the following sample is that of a forty-six-year-old man. We see firm strokes, heavy pressure and even

As a whole the writing is well proportioned. This graphic picture points to a vocation as a construction engineer, and one can surmise that this writer will be very successful in his field of endeavor. The numbers in the date lines are deftly written, revealing his talent for mathematics. The writer has a capacity for independent thinking and action and the ability to carry out his ideas. His emotional life, however, lags far behind his intellectual development. He is inclined to be selfish and unwilling to make any sacrifice or shoulder any obligation which might inconvenience him in any way. These traits are revealed by the fact that this script is much too narrow in proportion to the size. There are no final strokes, a characteristic which always reveals a lack of readiness to be considerate of others.

The following specimen is the script of a twenty-eight-year-old woman. The good form level, fluency, and speed, in addition to even spacing between words and lines, reveal this young woman's independence of thought and her high level of intelligence. This writer displays rhythm in her dynamic way of writing, which points to musical talent. She is alert and capable of expressing her thoughts intelligently and convincingly. Her emotional life, however, is somewhat disturbed and undeveloped. The double-curved ovals in the vowel "a" reveal inhibition and frustration. She has a strong feeling of inferiority and, despite her assets, doubts the adequacy of her native talents. This fact curtails her activities and makes her feel self-conscious and insecure. The warm pressure and rightward slant disclose her sanguine temperament, but she is prone to melancholy and depressive moods, as shown in the falling endings. In order to realize her potentialities to the fullest, this young woman needs to have her talents appreciated and confirmed by success in a career.

Dear Miss Marcuse

I would like you

something about my hand

Our new example is the wiry writing of a man of forty. It is much too narrow in proportion to its size, revealing a neurotic fear of the unknown. This rigid style of writing is characteristic of a person who is obstinate and hard to convince. All the "o's" and "a's" are tightly closed, some in duplication of an oval, disclosing the writer's secretiveness as well as his feeling of inferiority. In spite of his business dependability, fear and the negative attitude with which he approaches each undertaking handicap him and cause repeated failure. This man will never seek the reason for failure within himself, but has the habit of blaming either adverse circumstances or his business associates for his lack of success. The long lower loops reflect his materialistic greed. He appreciates only money. This man could be helped if he were willing to co-operate with those who are in a position to advise him. He should change his outlook on life, and have the courage and will to utilize his assets to the utmost by overcoming his negative attitude.

The following case is the exact opposite of our last. The author of this sample, also a man of forty, is jolly and full of hope and initiative. He will be a successful salesman, since he inspires confidence in his potential customers. The wavy writing, as well as the great speed, reveal an individual who is eloquent, who enjoys meeting people, and who is very approachable. The many interruptions between letters in several of the words disclose, however, that he concentrates with difficulty and that his attention wavers. This man is, by nature, sanguine, lively, restless, and seeks a continual change of activities. His shortcoming is that he "takes it easy," making promises which he cannot or does not always keep. However, he has the faculty of getting himself out of any difficulty. The threadlike connection in such a large writing is almost always indicative of unreliability. His greatest assets are his sense of humor and friendly disposition, which make him pleasant to meet. One is inclined to be lenient with his weaknesses.

Personnel Selection

In Germany handwriting analysis is widely applied in the industrial world. Many banks and great industrial firms use the services of graphologists. The chemical firm of I. G. Farben, for instance, never employs a single worker without having his handwriting analyzed. This proves an advantage also as a time-saver before interviewing people. In Switzerland, graphology is held in high esteem and widely applied in all branches of human endeavor. The same is true in England, France, Holland, Austria, Sweden and Norway. During the war, graphologists were employed to screen soldiers for efficiency, and for placement according to their ability.

In the United States, slowly but surely, the public is awakening to the usefulness of graphology. Mailing houses such as Spiegel and Montgomery Ward employ graphologists; their services have proved the usefulness of this method of character analysis. The services of handwriting analysts are sought and appreciated by many business firms which strive to overcome the problem of big turnovers in personnel. The United Seaman's Service of Personnel Selections has engaged Dr. Ulrich Sonnemann, author *of Handwriting Analysis as a Psychodiagnostic Tool,* in the capacity of a graphologist.

Usually the procedure for hiring a person to fill a vacancy is as follows. An advertisement is placed in one or two of the leading newspapers and handwriting applications are requested. The graphologist, called in for the examination of the specimen, is confronted with a great amount of material from which to choose. After a survey of the whole material, the specimens are classified in four groups: A, B, C, D. In most cases, only the first three are considered for interviews. The graphologist is told that the position calls for certain traits, such as intelligence, experience in the field, independence of action, knowledge of people, circumspection, emotional stability, and personality.

What is personality? In essence it is a subtle magnetism plus the trait of expansion in action. A person who is expansive projects himself into his social relationships; he talks readily, expresses his views frequently, and leaves little doubt as to his opinion on any subject. In short, he must be a positive, though not an aggressive, extrovert, possessing the social quality called tact. Investigation of the form level reveals his personality, intelligence, and versatility. Tempo is the clue to his way of work. Basic line reveals emotional stability and disposition. Such a survey is all we need to be able to judge the person justly.

Problems in Personnel Selection

There is at present a vacancy at the P ------ Company, a firm which handles men's clothing, wholesale and retail. The company is in need of an executive capable of supervising all the other branches in the city. The author of the attached sample has already been in-terviewed and is considered the right person for the position as far as experience, intelligence, and personality are concerned. Our task now is to check the findings and confirm the qualities expected.

The writer of this script, a man of forty, combines a good form level with some rhythmical disturbance. The handwriting is pri-marily released. It has a freedom of movement which implies a lively need for integration, and an attempt at overcoming the emotional disturbance. Nevertheless, the disturbance is substantial enough to cause unmastered inner controversies, impeding the writer in using his capacities to the utmost. While the speed is fast, even hasty but not consistently so, the pressure is uneven and at specific places, especially on the finals, displacement of pressure is present. The total movement is rather indicative of the writer's emotional instability. The threadlike connections also reveal here an additional inner conflict, sufficiently strong to interfere with a consistent attempt to formulate a goal and well-organized external pursuits. The highly unrhythmical breach in the central words presents a disquieting graphic appearance; in addition, the aimlessly lingering finals, which characterize an inner uncertainty of the writer, seem to confirm the fact that he is a sensitive person who is searching for consistent guidance. In spite of the writer's capacity to work well there is a possibility that he will break down under pressure.

The author of the next sample has also applied for the same position. A man of forty-eight, he is endowed with intelligence and good working habits (form level, regularity). He has a direct approach to life, is simple-minded, well-meaning and honest (form level, even spacing, rightward slant). In disposing of his work he exhibits enthusiasm, in addition to vigor and steadfastness of purpose (wavy t-bars, fluency). However, he is easily put out of humor, having the habit of fretting and worrying (no finals, personal pronoun "I" closed, some angular loops). He has decided views and strong convictions, but also narrow prejudices, which he obstinately defends (firm strokes, no change of slant, narrowness and tightly closed vowels). His disposition is unfortunate; he is jealous, distrustful of people, and tends to overwork because he lacks the ability to relax (uneven pressure, small letters unequal in size, writing looks crowded). His dependable character and trustworthiness are his assets. He also would work for the best interest of the firm and not for his own advantage (some garlands, no change of slant).

The writer of the next specimen, a man of forty, applies for a position as salesman. He is of average intelligence (form level), steady habits, is conscientious, and can be trusted (evenness of strokes, simplicity). He is conventional, with little initiative (narrow middle zone). He can be aggressive, but is usually patient and plans well (regularity, even spacing). He possesses acquisitiveness (long initial strokes with hooks). He is secretive and somewhat vindictive (vowels tightly closed, finals in "s" hooked). Ambitious, he has the will to succeed (firm strokes, even pressure).

A man of twenty-three has resigned his position and his employer wants to know the reason. His handwriting reveals that this man is intelligent and capable of working well, but is handicapped by being very wrapped up in himself (good form level, even spacing, narrowness, light pasty pressure, personal pronoun "I" closed). An

*I had planned to speak
week - but was unable to due to
I have made new plans for
Jan. 1st and I wish to give you
intention to resign.*

introvert to a degree of schizoid, he is always in doubt about himself. He is supersensitive, suspecting people's intentions toward him. Always suspicious, he feels constantly slighted.

*Enclosed you will find a resume
In response to your request, I am
observations. These are based on the short
during which I have been employed. My
limited to the budget department with who
familiar.
The budget department office has th*

The writer of the next sample is a man of twenty-three, and applies for a position as salesman in a store. He is of good intelligence and education (form level and even spacing). He is especially capable of attending to details, and is accurate and dependable (very small script, legible, i-dots and t-bars centered). He will be good at routine work, not having much imagination. He disposes of his work calmly, is honest and exacting (letters well hooked, equal size, no change of slant). He is a nervous type, but emotionally balanced. Being timid, he may be better for clerical work. However, since he is young, he may overcome this trait through experience.

A man of thirty-five applies for a position as salesmanager. The

In re your "ad" i
Sunday's Times, I would l
come in to see you to dis
the matter with you. If
telephone or write me, I w

good form level, even spacing, and fluency and originality of his writing reveals a man of high intelligence, initiative, and enterprise. His "t," appearing in the second and third lines, is a sign of executive ability and originality. He is independent in thought and actions and well-prepared for a high position by aptitude, personality, background, and training. The speedy writing shows activity and the ability to grasp essentials quickly. The even basic line discloses his emotional stability, while the emphasis of the lower zone reveals his material sense and good business ability. The personal pronoun "I" pictures a man of personality; one who is well-equipped to fill an executive position as salesmanager.

9.

Man and Woman in Marriage

All must recognize that any individual who binds himself to another in marriage must make concessions which may in a degree frustrate his own personality. But all social situations require give and take. In general, marriage assumes that both individuals must make reciprocal allowances in order to meet the wishes of the other party. Marriage certainly is not for extremely selfish people. Those who consider others' interests along with their own fare far more happily in marriage. Too often marriage is apt to become a habit, a life of routine. Husband and wife take each other for granted, and fail to do the little things which would make the other partner know that his part in the marriage is appreciated. As with other people, husband and wife should learn to give each other well-earned compliments, to show little courtesies, and to encourage each other's interests and activities.

In a well-matched marriage, many frustrations and ineptitudes which harassed the partners in their earlier lives may vanish. On the other hand, modern marriage itself presents many problems. To a great extent men have had to relinquish the idea of masculine dominance. Women want equality with men, but in this tendency they may easily go too far and become competitors instead of partners in the marriage. If both partners are emotionally well-balanced, if love and understanding are the leading motives in their relationship, differences can be easily bridged.

[handwriting sample — husband]

Dear Miss Marcuse,

I would like you to something about my hands

The two attached samples belong to a husband (upper) and wife (lower), both thirty-four-years of age. The man is an intelligent and educated person, as revealed in the good form level and even spacing. The warm pressure betrays the musician. The small size of the writing, with undefined letter formations, in addition to the uneven pressure, discloses his quick thinking as well as his unstable emotions. The heavy t-bars, together with the horizontal pressure, show temper and lack of control. The narrow script with tightly closed ovals reveal that he is absorbed in himself and has little understanding of others. Because of this unfortunate disposition he is not liked by other members of the orchestra. He therefore encounters some difficulty in finding employment, in spite of being a competent musician.

Then he met his wife, whose large, rounded writing reveals a warmhearted, maternal type of woman. Simplicity of letter forms show that she is free from complexity, and is honest and sincere. The man fell in love with her, believing that she would help him in overcoming his difficulties. Because they were basically not well-mated, their marriage turned out a failure, ending in divorce.

Physical inadequacies in marriage are a frequent reason for separation. If marriage continues merely for the sake of convenience, open or hidden tension may arise, making a harmonious relationship impossible. While physical attraction is important for a happy marriage, other vital factors involving the whole personality

must also be considered. Our first sample is that of a young man of twenty-three and the one following is that of a girl of the same age. Although they were aware of their temperamental difficulties they were attracted to one another and wished to marry. These two scripts immediately revealed the fact that both writers were frustrated as a result of early misunderstandings between their parents, shown by the ever-changing slant, backward slung lower loops, and general unsteadiness of letters. The young man's handwriting shows some independent letter forms and even spacing between words and lines, revealing a good intelligence and adequate educational training. After he has learned to organize and systematize his work better through experience, he should be able to succeed in a career. The heavy t-bars reveal that there is enough driving power and am-

bition to enable him to reach his goal. The open stems of the letter
"t" disclose his rather sensitive disposition. The hasty tempo, in addition to the many sharp angles, reveals his impatience, intolerance,
and irritability. However, the garland connections and warm shading
of the pressure show that he is warm-hearted and affectionate. In
spite of this, it would be quite difficult to live harmoniously with the
writer.

The young girl's handwriting does not display as good an educational background and intelligence as the young man's. However,
there is an emphasis on the upper zone, showing sufficient intellectual
meeting ground for her to adapt her interests to his. The garland
connections and lighter pressure disclose that she is affectionate, but
not quite as physically demonstrative as the young man. In the
change of slant we see that she is apt to be moody, tending toward
depression. On the whole, however, she is more even-tempered than
the young man. This couple were advised to wait and reconsider
their marriage, each meanwhile trying to work out his individual
problems. However, they did marry. The marriage did not work out,
because of the similarity of their frustrations and deficiencies of
disposition.

[handwritten sample:] "Well, folks, that about covers the write and tell us what you have be... for same. Sin Lore,"

Our next pair of samples belong respectively to a woman of twenty-seven and a man of twenty-eight. The slow tempo reveals a young woman of phlegmatic temperament and easy-going nature, who was an only child. The long initial strokes show her dependency on her parents to such an extent that she had little ambition to make her own decisions. The young man was also an only child. The lack of initial strokes, steadiness of letters, in addition to the firm pressure, are signs of his independence. When they were married, the girl transferred her dependency from her parents to dependency on her husband. Thus her dependence complements his assertiveness.

[handwritten sample:] "Will you kindly work on analyzing hand writ theme study, at your earliest"

[handwritten sample:] "I was very glad to, mee and I find that we have a very pleasant conversation"

When people of opposite temperaments marry there is a chance, as in the last case, that it may bring happiness. Unfortunately, the following case had less success. The first sample is that of a man of thirty-three who is bashful and shy. The very light pressure and uncertain strokes reveal this fact. The next sample, that of a woman of twenty-eight, shows rightward slant, fluency, and heavy pressure, revealing that the writer is vivacious and sociable. Although they thought their attributes complemented one another, marriage only exaggerated their differences. This is apparent in their scripts and could easily have been predicted by graphological analysis. In this case the marriage ended in divorce.

In the following case we have the handwriting of a man of twenty-two. That he is unsure of himself and an introvert is revealed by the double curved ovals and continual change of slant. The second sample, that of his wife, a girl of twenty, is vivacious, full of initiative and energy, shown in the speedy and fluent tempo with rightward slant, in addition to the heavy pressure. With her positive attitude toward problems, she inspires him to be firm, setting an admirable example for him to follow, without his being aware of the process. Their complementing natures built up their egos, making them important to each other.

Two fundamental causes for friction in marriage are sex and money. Since finances can be discussed more freely than sexual maladjustment, they may be often used to cover up such a conflict. Economic hardship does not, of necessity, create tension in marriage. Struggles shared sympathetically can bring a couple even closer together. In every marriage there are bound to be some differences. It is, therefore, wise to find ways and means to iron out such differences by open discussion. If resentment is smothered, it will eventually flare up, sometimes dangerously. But when difficulties are admitted and discussed, a solution can usually be reached in some amicable manner.

10.

Mental Disorder Expression

Without being mentally ill in a clinical sense, many persons are inhibited in the full use of their mental faculties by traits bordering on those of the psychotic. Psychoneurosis is always distinguishable from a psychosis by the fact that the patient is aware of his illness. Unlike the psychotic who is unsure of his delusions, and never able to comprehend how far astray from reality he is, the psychoneurotic is self-conscious, and comprehends to some extent at least his own disorder. His awareness of his condition makes co-operation possible and gives a valuable clue in determining whether the illness is psychotic or psychoneurotic.

Before discussing the psychoneurotic and psychotic, we may define mental health as the adjustment of human beings to their environment and to their fellow men. A mentally well-adjusted person recognizes his own limitations. He shows his mental health in part by frankly recognizing his intellectual limits. The normal person adapts himself, with a minimum of emotional energy, to the ever-changing pattern of living and refuses to be annoyed by petty inconveniences which interfere with his daily activities. His life is orderly, leaving his time and energy readily available for more important activities. He is not an extremist in the satisfying of any one desire. Instead, he strikes a balance in his deportment so that all ward the fulfillment of his aims are satisfied to the maximum and at the same time not to the detriment of others. These are the qualities of a well-adjusted personality; we realize of course that few people possess all of them. In short, mental health produces a well-rounded personality characterized by an interest in many things.

It is important to differentiate clearly between a neurosis, which is merely an unreasonable fight against reality, and a psychosis, which is a serious flight from reality.

Schizophrenia, in a clinical sense, is a term used to replace dementia praecox. It is a mental disease characterized by an extreme disorganization of the emotional life: hallucinations, fantastic delusions, and personality disintegration with relative intellectual preservation. It is the collective name for other manifestations of the diseased mind, the most frequent of which are manic-depressive and paranoia. The latter is a mental disease in which delusions of grandeur and especially of persecution play a dominant part. The individual feels that everyone, or at least one particular person, is set against him. Not only does he suspect that the world is antagonistic toward him, but he also believes that everyone is actually planning to harm, or even to destroy him.

A paranoid condition may develop either gradually and imperceptibly from early life, or may appear without warning in maturity. Becoming suspicious of what he believes to be the evil intentions of those around him, the paranoia withdraws from society until he has completely retreated into his own delusions. While the para-noia's mind is lost in the labyrinth of one particular delusion, his faculties, except when they touch his special delusion, remain quite normal. He may be obsessed with fixed and unwarranted suspicions about one person, and may yet be most logical and perceptive in all other respects. The paranoia who suspects the world at large may respond aggressively to his suspicion and become very dangerous.

Often delusions of grandeur rather than of persecution fill the mind of the paranoia; these resemble those of the manic state of the manic-depressive. He sees himself as an unquestionably distinguished personage. Paranoia and manic-depressive states may manifest themselves in an endless variety of confirmation of delusions. The manic-depressive passes from a state of elation to one of depression periodically without any tangible reason, in contrast to the normal moody person whose changes of mood are caused by exterior circumstances. In a state of elation, the patient may become extravagant in his actions, and thus irresponsible; in the depressive state he becomes sullen and seclusive.

We shall begin with handwritings of psychoneurotics, where we find those symptoms of mental imbalance which show in even more pronounced form in the handwritings of the psychotic. In the handwritings of all mentally unbalanced persons we observe a specific form of rhythmic disturbance, an increased inconsistency in the writing movement and extreme irregularity, in comparison to the display of the rhythmic quality described in the previous chapter. In manic-depressive personalities of considerable creativeness who are not clinically ill, this inconsistency is usually found together with a

high form level as shown in the attached sample. This is the script of a gifted musician and lecturer on music, a man of about forty. The good form level shows the writer's high intelligence and creative imagination. The undefined small letters, which present the basic line and middle zone, are unsteady and thready, too small in comparison to the other zones. The whole writing is loose and irregular, in addition to the disturbed rhythm in the writing movement. The overdevelopment of the upper zone reveals an exaggerated imagination; the overlong dashing t-bars disclose a lack of mental discipline; and the threadlike connections, with many disconnections, an inconsistency of thought. It shows a rapid even hasty, tempo which, in addition to the threadlike connection, discloses that the writer's thoughts are running away beyond control. The whole arrangement is still good and the spacing is fairly even, revealing a cultural background and excellent educational training. The lower loops are long but frail, disclosing that the writer does not have his feet on the ground. The case history was this: although the writer succeeded in obtaining a position in his field, his students realized that he often lacked coherence of ideas and complained of his rambling thoughts. After examination it was found necessary to hospitalize him for some time.

Our next case shows even greater mental confusion at first sight, but with study one realizes that the letters have more consistency and the pressure is even and heavy. The overcrowded and ill-spaced writing discloses the writer's disturbed inner experience. The fact that his confusion is not basic is revealed in the legible and angular script. The writer, a man of fifty, is a church organist of considerable talent, especially in improvisation. There is a warm shading in the pressure, and the tempo is fast without haste; this is shown by the fact that many letters are well-defined. As a whole, the writing displays complete lack of arrangement of space, which shows that the author is unaware of anything around him, due to his preoccupation with himself. The falling endings with entangled lines disclose the manic-depressive tendency in the state of depression. How little he is aware of what happens about him is revealed by the way he crowds the lines into the margins. He is considered peculiar by his colleagues, but is likable and innocuous. In spite of his talent, his mental condition makes him unfit to hold any position.

Dear Mrs Marcuse

I am very sorry I will not be able see for to morrow, Tuesday at 4.30, I do hope will understand, however I will be glad to see u any other time, and sincerely hope it will be y soon. With very best wishes

I remain   Sincerely

The next sample, that of a man of forty, betrays an unassuming nature and practical intelligence in the small script with even spacing between words and lines. The legibility and well-defined letters show his conscientious nature and ability to concentrate on his work as a bank clerk. The rightward slant shows that he tries to be friendly and sympathetic. The personal pronoun "I" attracts our attention because of its detachment from other letters and its vertical position. This important letter is also smaller than the other capitals, revealing the writer's inferiority complex; the narrow and compressed script with an unfirm stroke betrays a schizoid type of personality. The leanness of strokes and an empty, cold, and tedious stiffness reveal his shallow emotions, and also weakness of character which prevents him from assuming the responsibility to marry and raise children. There is a pronounced hesitancy in the whole writing movement which discloses his fear to venture courageously to build up his own life. It is as if he stood before an abyss in a strained attitude. The long, thin initial strokes reveal a negative attachment to the past. The abrupt final strokes show that something has made him lose his normal interest in others. He never achieved maturity and lacks any insight into himself or others. His neurotic fear has made him overly cautious, hesitant, and an escapist.

In the next case, the rightward slant and fluent script appears to belong to a person of open and sociable nature. However, we observe narrow letters and uneven, smeary pressure. It is a wiry script, with vowels tightly closed; the connections are mostly arcades running out into the thread. These graphic traits contradict our first impression of this thirty-year-old woman, because they reveal lack of insight into herself and others. In spite of the fluency and high degree of rightward slant with even spacing between words and lines, which point to logic and a clear mind, the writer, although of good intelligence, is undeveloped and emotionally immature. The lower loops are meager; in the first line in the word "looking," the "g" has a triangular lower loop which is unclosed. This is a clear sign of emotional and sexual frustration. The writer's desire to be affectionate is only conventional; she lacks courage and inner strength to follow her real nature. The arcade gives evidence of her conventionality and the thread corroborates our statement that she runs away from herself and her problems instead of solving them. All her sympathetic feelings are hidden behind a front of conventionality. There is a deep conflict in her nature which made her neurotic. She longs for companionship and love, but is hampered by the fear and inhibition which tend to hide her true nature. The smeary pressure reveals that her inner anxiety has also affected her physical condition, weakened it, and made it susceptible to all kinds of ailments. She is irritable, lonesome, and unhappy.

Normal development of the individual consists mainly of outgrowing childish attitudes, impulses, and feelings. In a classic passage, St. Paul expressed the test of maturity as do the psychiatrists of today: "When I was a child, I spoke as a child, I felt as a child, I thought as a child; but when I became a man I put away childish things." Normal maturity involves relegating infantile and childish attitudes and impulses to the past.

In our next case, a woman of forty has developed a severe paranoid condition. The script, in the unintelligible letter forms, displays a complete lack of concentration and reasoning powers. The smeary pressure, with edge-sharp terminals on letters such as "d" and "t" and t-bar crossings with sudden pressure, disclose the writer's violent aggressiveness and quarrelsome nature. There is little spacing between words, and the basic line is uneven and undulating, which betray this woman's confused mind. She has the fixed idea that she must protect herself from her mother who, she believes, is keeping her from seeing her friends. The rightward slant without any change reveals that she is still capable of attending to her duties in a millinery store, but the disturbed rhythm in the writing movement testifies to her mental imbalance. The case history revealed that she threatened several times to kill the mother with a knife. Since both shared an apartment, an immediate separation was recommended. The daughter was subsequently committed to an institution.

The next example displays a good adjustment of space, quick tempo, and a good form level, revealing an intelligent and educated woman of about thirty. The well-defined letters disclose efficiency and good perception. The lower, almost deteriorated, loops, however, show this writer's emotional immaturity. The sharp angle and pressure on occasional strokes disclose her uncontrolled temper and anger. The spacing between words is too wide in comparison to the small size of letters, revealing the writer's lonesomeness. There are drastic disconnections and continual change of slant even between letters of one word and the basic line is uneven. All these graphic traits point to an unstable and unpredictable person. The ovals are double-curved, which show that this young woman is always suspicious of everyone; and she fears being slighted by others. She is completely wrapped up in herself with little insight either into herself or others. The finals are abrupt, falling, with increased pressure; this shows disappointment and depression, the heavy pressure on these finals reveals that she will resent the supposed hostility of others and will become sarcastic even to the extent of mental cruelty. She is always tense and cannot seem to relax. This, in spite of her intelligence, will make her an unpleasant companion and she will have difficulty in making friends.

[Handwriting sample]

This oversized, loose script with light, uneven pressure reveals an eccentric woman. The slow and dashing t-bars are high up on the stem which, in addition to the inflated upper loops, show that the writer, a woman of middle age, is incapable of concentration and logic. The spacing is wide and uneven; in spite of the very large size, there are some threadlike connections, revealing the writer's lack of mental stability. The word "strange" in the fourth line indicates that she is subject to auditory hallucination. She identifies herself with that word, believing that her mission is to redeem the world. This word dominates the line, being completely different from its companions.

The open vowels in the letters such as "a" and "o" bespeak her talkativeness; she speaks incessantly of her impractical plans to anyone who will lend an ear. Through her delusive ramblings she makes a nuisance of herself. The hasty tempo and wide garland connections disclose her willingness and genuine desire to help her fellow men, but her readiness to do so is scarcely ever appreciated because of her hysterical and often foolish endeavors.

Personality disintegration can be defined by the extent of disintegration of graphic rhythm. Unduly abrupt or involved movements result from the disturbed mental functions of the writer. Abnormal graphic traits were visible only in a slight degree in the previous samples of handwriting. They become obvious in a more pronounced form in those which follow. The layman, as well as the graphologist, may be inclined to find these specimens rather orderly, with the exception of the writer's impaired ability to keep a straight line, a disproportion between height and width, and excessive wide-ness or narrowness which catch our attention.

The attached script is that of a middle-aged woman, diagnosed as suffering from stationary hypomania. Futile striving to resist her impulses is disclosed in increased irregularity, fancy curves, and connecting one word with the other, which is normally never found in scripts of such slow tempo. This woman was committed to a mental hospital for several years without any particular improvement. She seems always happy, exhibiting an elated state of mind, but paying little attention to her surroundings. Her only interest is listening to the radio and writing fan letters, such as this sample.

1. over XMas. I get down these days. g would hure t very much. It really is If you should feel it take a short trip came is Guilford 948, Jam

We now turn to the handwriting of a thirty-year-old man who is a manic-depressive psychotic. At the present state of insanity the depression is at the beginning of remission. The garland tendency is still noticeable; in addition to the high degree of rightward slant, this reveals a highly emotional person. The garland in this script is, however, low-saddled, called a "drooping" garland. This phenomenon, and the falling lines, mark the depression; the downward trend governs the picture of the depressed state. We also notice senseless disconnections in several words, such as "much" in the third line. Very obvious are the double-curved letters "d," "g," "a," etc. The uncertainty of the stroke, together with smeary pressure, reveals the writer's confused thoughts. This man is of good intelligence and education, as revealed by the good form level and fairly even spacing. At this state of remission the slow tempo begins to accelerate; the whole movement, however, is distorted and unrhythmic. The patient has been in a mental hospital for some time. He was willing to be committed because he realized that he was incapable of coping with life and its problems.

In the following sample paranoid schizophrenia is marked by the neglect of the horizontal connections of letters such as in the first word "Woul-d," and in the second line "h-ave," in addition to an extreme expansiveness of letters, sharpness, and artificial fullness. All these signs characterize auditory hallucination. The active aggressiveness in this woman's script is disclosed in the heavy and sharp t-bars and in all endings. The angularity is needle-sharp, which makes the diagnosis of this handwriting comparatively easy. This woman has the fixed idea of grandeur. She believes she is of royal heritage, and likes to behave as a queen and give commands. The personal pronoun "I" shows her self-aggrandizement in the inflation of size.

Mrs. Irene Mancuso
243 West 100th Street
New York City

My dear Marcuse

Enclosed please find,
for Selma's piano recital. Ito
to see you and say hello to you

While the manic-depressive shows considerable speed in the manic state, the depressive state shows increase in slowness, as in our next sample. This handwriting, of a stationary depressive psychotic, a man of fifty-five, reveals mental imbalance by the slowness and unfirm stroke of the pen. The pressure is light and uneven with some smeary spots, as if the writer lacked the courage to lift the pen. The basic line is uneven; all the vowels are involved and ink-filled. There are again senseless disconnections in words. The first word "En-clo-sed" is torn into two parts as if they did not belong together. "Pi-ano" in the second line shows the same separation. There is a continual change of slant in the whole script; in addition to the drastic disconnections, this reveals incoherence of thought to such an extent that the writer is not aware of what he says or does. This man was a lawyer, but was unable to carry on his profession; he was declared irresponsible. Although harmless, he disrupted his home life to such an extent that he was committed to a mental hospital.

Dear Madam

I hope you will analyze my handwriting

Our last sample reveals an incipient state of paranoia. It is the script of a young man of twenty-five, a musician of great talent. In spite of his intelligence, he betrays himself by uneven spacing between words; the basic line shows extreme unevenness, and the writing lacks rhythm and regularity. The smeary pressure with edge-sharp endings reveals paranoia. This young man was always considered peculiar, but excused because of his great talent. He was able to practice his instrument and play in public. His psychotic condition became obvious only when he was inducted into the army. At first, he could not stand the discipline and rebelled; later he complained of being persecuted by certain soldiers. He was examined and committed to an army mental hospital where he remained about three years. In his discharge, he was declared mentally incompetent. He continues his musical career, but is not capable of holding any position.

Clinical graphology is only in its beginning stage. The investigator must be continuously aware of the many dangers involved in a proper analysis in view of the number of overlapping concepts in psychiatry itself. It is not the task of the graphologist to diagnose, but only to confirm, by examination of graphic traits, the different expressions of mental disturbance.

11.

Criminal Tendencies

We know of two types of criminals; the courageous type, who dares to be a successful antagonist of society, and the frustrated type, who cannot find another way, due either to indolence or inability to adjust to difficult situations.

It is generally assumed that the mind regulates behavior. This leads to the inquiry as to which mental deviations or mental abnormalities have to do with criminal behavior. Is there a relationship between the criminal's mental make-up and the crime? Can it be supposed, in certain cases, that the criminal's personality has deviated so far from the normal that there is present an underlying pathological factor which prompts the crime? The investigations of Cesare Lombroso (who also studied the handwriting of the criminal), and to Freud and his followers, have probed deep into the human mind. These scientists have also studied the factors which motivate human behavior and the ulterior forces which seem to urge men into crime.

As will be seen in the following cases, a comprehensive knowledge of personality is often one of the keys, or the key, to behavior which otherwise defies explanation. A man may not show gross mental abnormalities, but nevertheless be driven into crime by an unconscious urge.

Each criminal is compelled toward his own type of crime, depending upon his personality and the circumstances of his existence. A person of low intelligence will, in most cases, commit a simple offense, such as stealing some insignificant object. A highly intelligent individual will commit a more complicated crime. Any criminal act is fundamentally determined by the personality of the perpetrator. Experience has furnished ample proof that those with strength of character will not be tempted into crime, even under trying circumstances.

All human judgments of value and success are ultimately founded upon man's desire to co-operate. This is the great shared commonplace of the human race. We shall never find a man who is completely devoid of social feeling. The neurotic and the criminal also know this open secret. We can see this fact in the effort they make to justify their way of life or to shift responsibilities elsewhere. They have lost courage, however, to proceed in the constructive side of life. They have turned away from its real problems and are engaged in shadow-boxing to reassure themselves.

We shall begin our analyses by considering a script the interesting symbols of which reveal that the writer, a man of thirty-five, has the active guilt-complex of a neurotic. One day this man had a heated argument with his mother, who was a nagging paranoia, after which she suffered a fatal heart attack. He felt that he was responsible for her death. This was due to the fact that he had never been able to deny a feeling of resentment toward his mother and often actually wished her dead. The writing presents some peculiarities, such as the detached letter "T" in the third line, and the personal pronoun 'I' at the beginning. Most conspicuous and pictorial, however, is the canopy ending his first name William, which is almost like a hand pointing back to some impressive part of his past, which his "subconscious" symbolically pictures in the writing. The thread-like connections corroborate this trait, disclosing that the writer is running away from something in his past or from himself. Although this man was not actually a criminal, he believed himself to be one, and not until he saw clearly his mistake was he entirely freed of fear and self-condemnation.

They will furnish excellent references, no object and I am to satisfy you.

Our next case involves the handwriting of a seventeen-year-old boy who applied for a position as shipping clerk in a textile concern. The large and widely written script, with heavy pressure, discloses the boy's laziness and easy-going nature. The even spacing between words and lines reveals his intelligence and his clear, logical mind. The conspicuous, inflated lower loops, with strong pressure on the down strokes, disclose his gross, avaricious, and prematurely over-sexed nature. The firm and heavy pressure reveals the boy's physical strength. He is capable of doing his work well, since he has the necessary drive and ambition. However, he wants success and the good things of life without any effort. The large, loose writing together with a change of slant denotes weakness of character. He followed the line of least resistance, resorting to petty thievery, and was caught. His home environment was not conducive to the development of strong character traits. Weak and well-meaning parents are often amazed when confronted with their offspring's derelictions.

Let us note for further reference that it is not always defined criminal tendencies which cause the individual to commit a crime. Weak character is the basis for most deviations in both the youthful and adult personalities. Early prevention, instead of attempted cure, should be the paramount issue, as we shall see in the following case.

This twenty-one-year-old girl's handwriting discloses in the fairly even spacing between words, and in the medium tempo, an average intelligence. The high degree of rightward slant reveals an over-emotional nature, while the pasty and smeary pressure shows the tendency to indulge in her sexual desires. The letters vary in size; the small letters are hardly legible, revealing the writer's un-truthfulness and dishonesty. The angularity runs out into a thread, a type of writing which is characteristic of those who cannot be relied upon. The parents mentioned that the girl had had affairs at an early age. The handwriting betrays her voluptuousness in the smeary pressure and fat lower loops. Later, while she was employed as salesgirl in a department store, a large theft was discovered. This girl was suspected, and found guilty, not only of this theft, but of stealing money from the cash register. She was sentenced to prison. Her parents did not realize that, where they had sowed overindulgence and lack of understanding, the result would be so devastating. The twenty-three-year-old man's handwriting reproduced below reveals average intelligence and education. The letters are

Dear Mrs. Marcuse,

I have asked Walter if I
to you to have my handwriting
He suggested that you may be
me determine the type of work
I would be most adapted.

formed after the school model, displaying little individuality. The spacing between words is fairly even, disclosing that the writer, possesses reasoning power. The heavy pressure is conspicuous. However, on close examination, it is apparent that it does not flow, but is cramped and blocked on the down strokes. In addition to this peculiarity, there are negative disconnections in several words. All these graphic traits disclose the writer's addiction to alcohol, and his lapse of memory, in addition to inconsistency in his personality. Although this young man is able to play several different band instruments, he is so unreliable that he cannot hold a position/Despite the rhythmical fluency which characterizes musicianship, the tempo of this script is slowed down at many points. The size of all letters is not maintained, which points to the fact that he is weak in character and lacks the will to conquer his continuous craving for liquor. It is only fair to say that he has been cured of alcoholism through a genuine and lasting spiritual regeneration, and is now leading a useful life.

you are out of ꭱey for the
I will you be there? next

The handwriting of our next specimen belongs to a man of thirty-six. We notice that the pressure is inconsistent and light; at times some pressure is added, especially on the upper loops. The writer is less concerned here with the content of what he writes than with making a good impression by his handwriting. In his zeal, he exaggerates the embellishments and gives the script an artificial look. Another peculiarity is apparent in the large and double-curved ovals as in the small "o." This is a clear indication of deception and dishonesty. The continual change of slant in this rather large script is a sign of evasiveness and chicanery. For the most part, this writing is connected, disclosing that he possesses the faculty of clear reasoning. The uneven spacing between words, however, shows that he had never been trained to make the most of his native intelligence.

This writer was completely immoral. He had run away from home when fourteen and made a living in various ways, at times with some success. At other times he tried an easier way by swindling women, who often helped him financially. This large writing, with letters of uneven size, betrays the writer's weakness of character and love of an easy life, with no attempt to help himself. The light and uneven pressure is that of a lazy and weak-willed person. He is a "wishful thinker" and a "poor doer." He never learned to assume responsibility and never acquired an honest attitude in dealing with his fellow men.

As we have discussed at greater length in chapter ten dealing with mental disease, the types of mental disorder most frequently found in criminals are the psychosis in combination with mental deficiency; those related to the use of alcohol and drugs, schizophrenia, manic-depressive psychosis and psychopathic inferiority. Mental illness seems to be significant in the cases of crime in three ways: (1)

where delusions of persecution lead the individual to attack his imagined persecutor; (2) where the psychosis has the effect of excluding a patient from relationships which give him status, for which he compensates by attention-getting behavior; (3) where the psychosis is a substitute for crime in an intolerable life situation—a flight from reality as an alternative to criminal outbursts.

Neurotics, constitutionally psychopathic inferiors, and epileptics are discovered in varying numbers among criminals. Neurotics, unable to compete satisfactorily in society, may resort to crime. The unbalanced egocentric is variously estimated to be responsible for more or less crime. Some psychiatrists consider the fact of conviction of crime evidence of a psychopathic personality. The implication is that psychopathic criminals are involved in a disproportionate number of violent acts.

My Darling Baby,

I love you very much. Darling, when

Our next example is the handwriting of a twenty-eight-year-old man who murdered his sweetheart, whom he suspected of infidelity. He planned the crime in detail and executed it with deft cruelty. We notice edge-sharp endings, continual change of slant, senseless disconnections and thread, which sum up the unpredictable and violent actions of the aggressive paranoia.

In our next case, we notice the distorted letters with continual change of slant and an uneven basic line. In this case, the person focused upon as the cause of persecution was the writer's employer. He was found in his employer's office after closing time, having demolished the entire place, setting fire to papers on the desk, and causing great damage. The final verdict in this case was criminal insanity, making it necessary to commit the writer to an institution.

[handwritten sample: "I just spoke to your Lilian - she is tired from too much work - and running around - week ends Best regards"]

The manager of a great business concern for which I regularly worked, called upon me to examine twenty samples of handwriting because a tremendous theft was discovered and I was to find which of the employees might come under suspicion. After close investiga-

[handwritten sample]

tion of the submitted scripts I pointed to the above sample, whose author seemed to me the only one who was capable of committing a crime. The manager of this employee's department protested strongly, explaining that this man was unquestionably honest and a very efficient worker whom he had known for some time. According to this handwriting, the man undoubtedly is intelligent and efficient, but my attention was attracted to the many mendings of strokes, es-

pecially in the numbers, in addition to covered up strokes, such as in
"s," "a," "d." Such mending of letters is a sure sign of dishonesty,
especially in such a fluent handwriting as this. Just as it was difficult
to detect this writer directly as a criminal, his handwriting presents
the same difficulty because of the clever concealments of strokes,
which are visible only to an experienced eye. My suggestion was to
watch the man closely without arousing his attention. This was
done, and about six months later there was sufficient evidence of his
criminal actions. He obstinately defended himself (angular "y"),
but to no avail. Solving this case was a great satisfaction to me because of the extreme difficulty of discovering the criminal.

This sample is the handwriting of a fifty-three-year-old man
who was arrested on narcotic charges, being himself addicted to a
drug. The light pressure and inflated lower loops with almost no
pressure, indicate the drug addict. There is little resistance in this
man; almost all connections are threadlike and the middle zone is

unsteady. His emotional confusion is shown in entangled lines; the whole writing presents a picture of weakness of character and lack of consistency. The form level is above average; the writer is endowed with good intelligence and quick perception. However, he is unreliable and untrustworthy. Although he displayed a desire to change his condition, he never was able to keep any promise, and finally became involved with a narcotic ring.

Conclusion to Part I

We have demonstrated that knowledge of personality, intuition, and practical wisdom are needed in analyzing each individual's handwriting. Our endeavor has been to present the subject of graphology in such a way that our readers will have gained sufficient knowledge to direct themselves, and to help those around them. We feel that the chapters on technique will serve as a textbook for both private students and those who have completed a correspondence course.

Analysis of one's own handwriting opens the door to self-analysis, which in turn can lead to the fulfillment of life for each one of us.

The Bible says, "Where there is no vision, the people perish." We must attain understanding of ourselves and our neighbors in order to reach the goals of tolerance and progress. In the growth of each of us into mental and emotional maturity lies the hope of our world.

PART II. THE GREAT MUSIC-MASTERS
AS PORTRAYED IN THEIR HANDWRITING

12.

The Classic Period

My musical interest first led me to a special investigation of musical genius as portrayed in handwriting. As the work progressed my interest became centered in their personalities.

Before entering on our discussion of these studies let us try to clarify what genius is. Undoubtedly a genius must be original. Emerson says: "Every great man is unique;" and George Eliot declares: "Genius comes into the world to make new rules."

A genius is an exalted intellectual power capable of operating independently of tuition and training, and marked by extraordinary faculty for original creation, invention, discovery and expression. Genius is greater than talent, more spontaneous, less dependent upon instruction, less amenable to training. It may be said that a genius is a person of phenomenal powers.

In analyzing the handwritings of the musical genius let us distinguish and define two important psychological classifications: the classical genius and the romantic genius.

The classical genius is complete in himself and has purpose; he is intent upon production, rather than indulgence in phantasies. He is never flighty and holds his passions in strict control. The classical type is a master of rigorous form, while the romantic often shatters all bonds of the rules of art. The latter often works spasmodically. He can be called lazy because he works only when in the mood. He is more fluid in type than the classical genius, secures his ideas with less effort, works in the fire of enthusiasm and generally has greater intuition.

The classical genius, as a rule, produces his work relatively late in life and can be called the more solid of the two types. The romantic genius is of the suffering type — melancholy, excitable, erratic; the classical genius often lives apart from people and works hard. The ideal of the classical composer is predominantly an intellectual one, producing works characterized by clearness and symmetry, by harmonious proportion, by simplicity and repose.

It is extremely difficult, almost impossible, to define clearly the nature of these two types of genius. Their character traits often overlap, and only when the traits of either type predominate, can one speak of a definite romantic or classical attitude. In a minor degree, though not apparent, both influences may affect the artistic and psychological attitude of both geniuses. This can be traced through all the various phases of their musical expressions.

In this investigation I shall go back ho further than to the early eighteenth century, because this is an epoch which is musically of the greatest importance. ·

Johann Sebastian Bach and Frideric Handel represent this epoch: both bring the baroque to a definite close, exemplifying the spirit of their age and personifying the climax. Although these two geniuses generally are classified together, they are as different in their artistic tendencies and achievements as in their personalities.

JOHANN SEBASTIAN BACH

Bach's handwriting reveals strongly his empathy with the meaning of the written word. His thinking is objective; his thoughts are embodied and made visible in his handwriting. I noticed that Bach's handwriting in the marginal notes and words to many of his

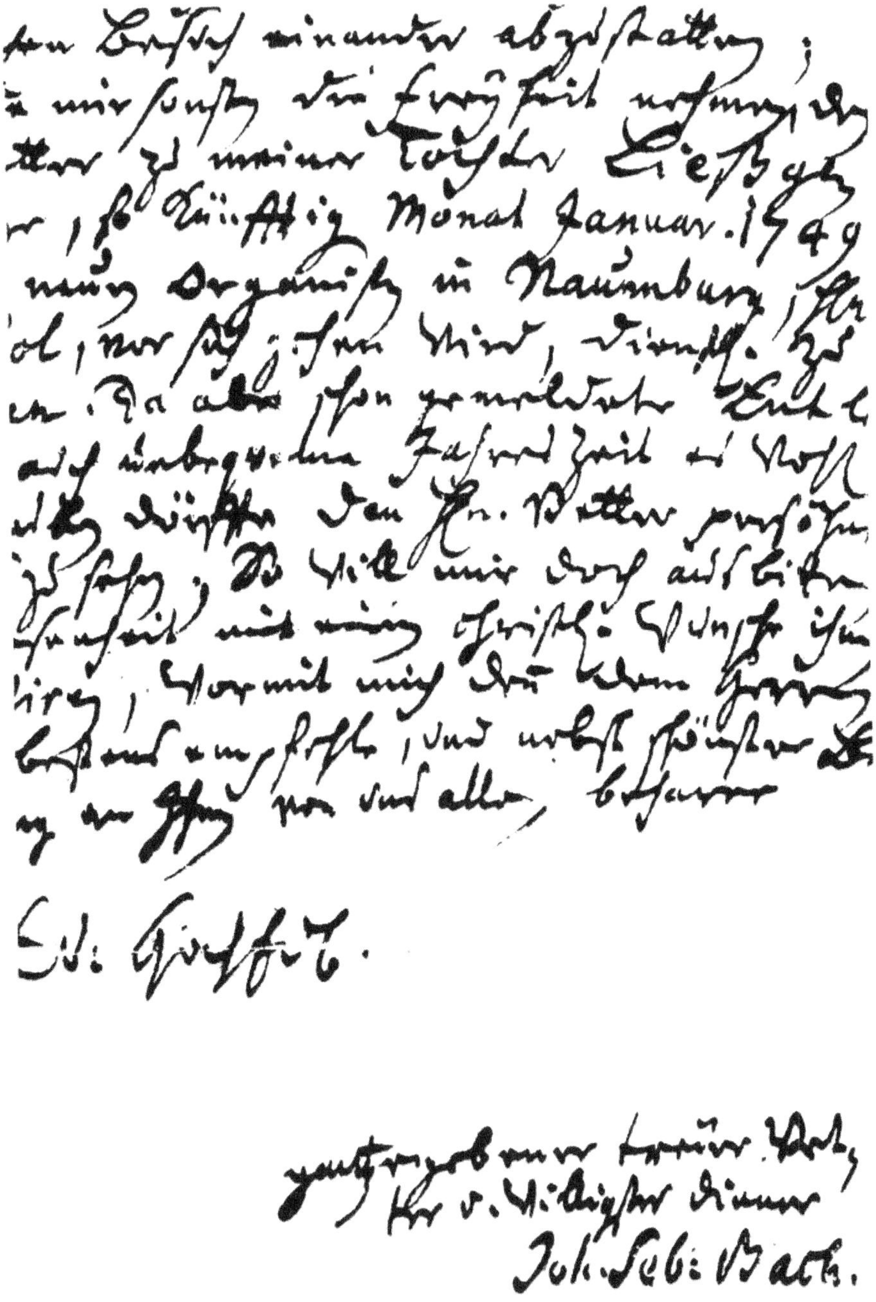

masses, cantatas, and chorals varied in form to match the music. When he was setting down a slow, quiet movement, his handwriting was even and regular; when he came to a lively movement, or a particularly impassioned section, his handwriting clearly showed the emotional stress under which he was working.

In all his manuscripts we recognize an imaginative strength and a singular energy, disclosed in the heavy and even pressure on the down strokes. A man who can draw such lines must possess an inexhaustible drive toward accomplishment.

In his nature Bach combined simple modesty, industry and good humor with the sensitivity, intellectual curiosity and hot-blooded temperament of the highest type of artist. The first three qualities are reflected in the simple, unadorned letter forms, as well as in the emphasis on the upper zone; the heavy, warm shading of the pressure reveals his temperament.

His fervor, penetration and vast imagination shown in his interpretation of the Holy Scriptures are revealed by this stress on the upper zone and by the pressure. The ascending trend of letters uncovers his whole conception of life and the world, which is based on his faith in God, from whom comes his spiritual strength. The emphasis is on the size of the upper zone, while the lower is only indicated, revealing that' the materialistic world seems unimportant in comparison to his highly developed spiritual life. Bach was free of the jealousy and envy that beset many musicians, always generous in his admiration of his fellow composers. This generosity is reflected in the relatively long terminals of his small writing.

The study of the style of handwriting in use at the time of Bach shows that he has not created a new style of writing, but uses the contemporary style in a new and original manner. Bach's handwriting gives us a clue to his compositions. The fact is that he conforms to the handwriting style of his time and from this we learn that Bach was not concerned with overthrowing any of the generally accepted fundamental maxims, but merely with varying their manner of expression. His ambition was not to create a new style in music, but rather to perfect the existing one. The ideal for which he fought with unswerving zeal, and to which he dedicated his life, brought him repeatedly into conflict with those in authority over him, who tried to impose on him their mediocre standards.

In the firm and heavy hooks of the German "t" Bach's great pride is revealed. He has been called obstinate and pugnacious, but the truth is that he never asked anything for himself. He asked only to be allowed to make music.

.FRIDERIC HANDEL

HANDEL also follows the contemporary style of handwriting. Handel also does not deviate. His genius, like Bach's, is mirrored in the original fashion by which he modifies the accepted style. One cannot speak of any revolutionary spirit in this script.

While Bach's writing is rather vertical, Handel's shows a high degree of rightward movement, disclosing his outgoing nature, that

of the extrovert. Bach was satisfied with an intimate circle of friends, had no ambition to reach the great public, but wished only to serve the church to the glory of God. Handel, on the other hand, as the typical extrovert, wanted to address the whole world. He was the dramatist. The first letter, capital V, pictures the composer's desire to reach out to the world. It makes a great bow to the public. His desire for publicity and admiration is mirrored only in this letter V. The signature is simple, unadorned, and yet imposing in its individuality. Although devoid of the flourishes which we often find in the handwriting of his contemporaries, there is a certain, pageantry in this very simplicity, reminding us of a painting by Rubens.

Handel could afford to be modest, because he was conscious of his genius and sure of himself and his fame. Therefore he had no need to embellish his letters, especially those of the signature, nor to impress the public by underscoring it. The graceful leftward bow of letters such as "d", reveals the same perfect sense of form and beauty shown in his musical compositions.

His opportunity for many effects with grand chorus of which the virile and dramatic-minded Handel could fully avail himself in ways peculiarly native to his genius, is revealed in the individual shading of pressure in the horizontal direction and in the impressive capitals.

CHRISTOPHER WILLIBALD VON GLUCK

Christopher Willibald von Gluck's style of handwriting presents a change from the baroque to the rococo. There is less pageantry than in Handel's writing, but instead, an intimate charm

in the small and graceful movements of the pen, especially in the backward bow of the small "d" and the capital letters "M" in Monsieur and "V" in Vienna.

The script shows the third dimension, which gives depth to the whole. Gluck's writing is less pictorial than that of Bach and Handel. The deeply-saddled garland connections together with the warm shading of the pressure reveal Gluck's sensitivity to sound and a new emotional expressiveness. This emotional force enabled him to make wonderful new discoveries in the invention of melody.

The superior form level and beautiful sense of proportion displayed in the writing reflect Gluck's creative genius. He follows the powerful impetus of his innate musical instinct. Through the noble simplicity and purity of his compositions we see mirrored the elegant and symmetric arrangement of these clear and simplified letters.

JOSEPH HAYDN

Joseph Haydn's script reveals a new style, new aesthetic creeds, a revolution in art. The freedom of movement in this new style of writing foretells the romantic emotionalism of Beethoven.

Considering that the rococo epoch was on the whole effeminate, Haydn's writing discloses an almost robust, masculine type, in spite

of its small size and flourished letters. The smallness discloses Haydn's capacity for concentration, and the firm and heavy pressure, his masculine energy. All that charm which is pictured by minute detail in his compositions seems to be expressed in these graceful letters. His great sense of humor and fun is displayed in the wavy final stroke of his signature. It is a pictograph expression of Haydn's humorous way of making faces when any occasion called for such fun. The long final stroke also symbolizes his kindly and sociable nature and his love for his fellow men. ^

The heavy horizontal pressure explains his devotion to his work for its own sake, without any seeking for personal aggrandizement. The beautiful arrangement of the whole script and the afore-mentioned sense of proportion, exemplify the noble structure of his music.

WOLFGANG AMADEUS MOZART

Wolfgang Amadeus Mozart's handwriting displays a genuine elegance free from hypocrisy. In spite of the gallantry and superficiality of the rococo period, there is no futile flourish in this elegant script, but an adornment which is deeply rooted in the composer's nature. His great sense of proportion, which is apparent in the artistic arrangement of the script, is a symbol of his way of composing. There is neither one bar too much nor too little. It is as

though he builds a house which is neither too large nor too small and then furnishes it in perfect taste.

Mozart's writing reveals a remarkable strength of character in contrast to all the artificiality which is typical of that age. Since the general trend of the rococo period was decadent during Mozart's life, his genuine gracefulness and sincerity must be regarded as a special sign of pure artistic expression.

Mozart does not attempt to cast aside this delicate style of his time, but he utilizes all its grace and brings it to a climax. We know that Mozart died on the threshold of a new era. The age which died with him finds its most enchanting and delightful expression in his music.

The warm shading of the pressure, in addition to the rightward slant, reflects his great love for mankind. The handwriting is small and concentrated, revealing his love for detail. We observe letters climbing gracefully into the upper zone, the realm of the spiritual and creative imagination. The lower zone also is well-emphasized, disclosing that Mozart's chief emotional expression is erotic to a far greater extent than in any composer before or after him. In this emphasis of the lower zone his attraction to the opposite sex and his passionate nature are clearly pictured.

The writing runs across the page to the right without inter-ruption, at full speed, revealing the fertility of his imagination in composition, and also his lively temperament and acute sensibility.

Mozart's profound faith in God and his inclination toward things spiritual are shown in the round and high i-dots. His melan-choly tendency is visible in some falling endings. However, the writing at times displays an upward trend, revealing that his inner harmony and his faith in God do not permit him to dwell on tragic themes. The highly dynamic writing, in addition to the superior form level, discloses Mozart's tremendous genius.

One cannot fail to notice in the handwritings of Haydn and Mozart, that both obviously are related to each other in style, al-though it is easy to those who are familiar with the period to dis-tinguish between them.

Just as the period prescribes a particular kind of gesture, the musical fashion of an epoch leaves its stamp upon musical style. While both Haydn and Mozart benefited from the same culture, each of them reached the pinnacle of success by diversified paths, as may be seen by these handwritings of the geniuses.

LUDWIG VAN BEETHOVEN

Compared with the handwritings of Gluck, Haydn and Mozart, who lived in the pre-French revolutionary period, Beethoven's way of writing is less bound by the scholastic form of script used in his

day. This symbolizes his breaking away from former traditions to create a new style.

As a follower of the French revolutionary tradition, Beethoven exhibits that spirit by omitting all flourishes. Judging by the appearance of this script it looks almost modern, revealing to us how far ahead of his time Beethoven was.

The writing displays an exceptional form level, in addition to tremendous speed and dynamic movements. The ever changing size of the letters discloses his inner restlessness. This explains his creative method.

The pressure, though heavy, is transposed from the down strokes to the side strokes. This transposition of pressure reveals that Beethoven put all his energy and activity into his work, with no thought of personal ambition.

This unequal size of letters also expresses his over impulsiveness and his high-strung temper. His great humanity and emotionalism are expressed in the high degree of rightward slant and in the garland connections.

The freedom and originality displayed in this fluent writing are the graphic reflection of a genius who knew no limitations, and went his own way unmoved by public opinion.

The little flourish adorning his signature epitomizes his fine sense of humor.

FRANZ SCHUBERT

Like the handwriting of Beethoven, Schubert's script reflects the outstanding ideas of his age, but as his writing shows the great difference in form quality and dynamic expression, we realize that

Schubert's reaction to the problems of the day differs considerably from that of Beethoven.

The high-climbing upper extensions of letters reveal Schubert's gift of inexhaustible melody, which no other composer ever surpassed. The well-defined and legible script discloses that he is constantly striving to make himself understood.

The dynamic swing and fluency of these firm letters with heavy pressure display the boldness of his youthful energy and creative activity. There is much buoyancy in the careful drawing of these lines reflecting his great passion for detail.

Enthusiasm, inspiration and idealism are disclosed in the clearly dotted "i's" which are flying ahead of letters. The clearness and steadiness of his letters reveal Schubert's inner self-assurance which is mirrored in all his compositions.

13.

The Romantic Period

Before leaving the classical period, let us summarize what we have learned from the examples cited of the classical traits exhibited by these composers which we translated into graphological terms. The handwritings did not present any unnecessary ornamentation, but remained simple in character, in spite of great speed and fluency.

We now approach the period of the exponents of the romantic school. Graphologically we shall observe fewer of those characteristics which we found in the writings of the classical period.

The intermingling of classical and romantic traits can be clearly observed in the handwritings of Carl Maria von Weber, Felix Mendelssohn, Robert Schumann, Frederick Chopin, and Johannes Brahms.

CARL MARIA VON WEBER

Weber's handwriting runs across the page with feverish activity at tremendous speed. His facility in composing is clearly expressed in the threadlike connections, disclosing the rapidity of his thought. In spite of this velocity there is power and balance in the steady basic line and in the even spacing between words and lines.

The elegance and charm displayed in the dashing finals, in addition to the emphasis on the upper zone, reflect Weber's beauti-

ful creative imagination and originality. These flying movements of the pen are different in shape from those we encountered in the writings of the classical period. The writing becomes less formalized, and is adorned with flourishes, a characteristic of the romantic imagination. The small adornment at the end of Weber's signature reveals his romantic nature.

FELIX MENDELSSOHN BARTHOLDI

Felix Mendelssohn Bartholdi's script displays the romantic spirit in the rich flourishes throughout the whole writing. When we compare the flourishes of Mendelssohn's script with those of Mozart and Haydn we gather the impression that Mozart's flourishes are intended deliberately. They are incorporated into the basic structure without changing its fixed style. The flourishes of Weber and Mendelssohn, on the other hand, look like mere decorations, written spontaneously, and in an impulsive manner.

With Mozart and Haydn the flourishes are a necessary part of the formation of the letters, which would not be legible without them. In the writings of Weber and Mendelssohn, the flourishes are just an adornment, characteristic of their romantic imagination.

Felix Mendelssohn's script is classical in its style shown by the steadiness and regularity on the one hand, and on the other, highly romantic expressed in the many flourishes. It is a romanticism that

is not in the least morbid, but colorful and sparkling. He is both classical and romantic: a symbol of the transition between two epochs.

Mendelssohn's script displays large and fluent movements of the pen, revealing his great enthusiasm and the fertility of his creative imagination. Superior intelligence and culture are shown in the superior form level and in the well-defined letters. The delicacy of his sentiment is mirrored in the fascinating contour of the small letter "d," which bows elegantly backward. His pride and firmness of character are displayed in the angular style. The beautiful adornment at the signature reflects his talent for painting and drawing.

ROBERT SCHUMANN

Robert Schumann's creative imagination dominates his whole personality. The speed and fluency of this writing, in addition to its unique letter forms, presents the incarnation of the romantic spirit and of Schumann's poetic nature, which lifts him above the commonplace.

The script is very small, revealing not only his fine gift for picturing intimate scenes in music, but also his introvert nature, which seeks escape into a world of fantasy.

The good proportion of this writing, as well as its originality in the connection of letters, mirror the writer's poetic exaltation and his deep understanding of romantic feeling.

The warm shading of the pressure, which is transposed into the side stroke, discloses his creative emotional power, and the purity

and sincerity of his feeling. However some brittle strokes and a wavering basic line reveal some weakness and emotional instability.

In spite of this instability, which can also be observed in the structure of some of his compositions, his emotional force is so great that it overpowers this structural weakness.

Schumann's emotional power is so irresistible that it has not lost its magic even after a century.

FRÉDÉRICK CHOPIN

Frederick Chopin's handwriting is remarkable for its simplicity. This simplicity reveals him as a fastidious artist with a strong creative imagination. It also shows us his exclusiveness. But this latter characteristic is somewhat counterbalanced by the high degree of rightward slant, which, in addition to the garland style, mirrors his

emotional intensity. This combination of characteristics may seem paradoxical; yet, this desire for seclusion with a simultaneously warm sympathy for his fellow men, are typical of Chopin's personality.

The very light pressure shows Chopin's supersensitivity and the instability of his moods. The delicacy of the letter formation reflects his pure feeling and his somewhat feminine and highly impressionable reaction to sentiment; it also reveals his romantic nature.

On the other hand, the simplicity, clearness and legibility of his script, as well as the evenness of the pressure, reveal his masculine energy and perseverance. The superior form level and even spacing between words and lines disclose Chopin's superior intelligence and logical mind. The i-dots are high and clear and the upper zone is emphasized revealing his idealism and inspired thought.

His signature is slightly underscored, showing that, although Chopin is modest, he is well aware of his great and important position in the musical world.

The whole writing pictures Chopin as an independent thinker. His Polish background may be traced in some letters, as for instance, the capital "M" in the second line, which reveals his nationality. This is only a minor item which in no way contradicts his cultural universality.

JOHANNES BRAHMS

The romanticism in Johannes Brahms's script is revealed by the number of large movements of the pen, but there is at the same

time a steadiness in these letters which is a clear expression of the classical spirit.

Brahms started his artistic career with romantic impetuosity, which was later curbed by an ever-growing reverence for the art of the great classical masters.

The small letters, with some graceful bows, such as the small "h" and "z," reveal the lyric spirit of the writer, the intimacy of his mode of expression and his reticence.

We must realize that a composer of such powerful personality is capable of expressing himself in both the dramatic and lyric style. The word "Triumphlied" shows Brahms, the dramatist, in its powerful first letter.

The pressure is heavy both in words and notes, although it is transposed into the side strokes, revealing that Brahms worked out all his passionate feelings into his music.

Purity, sincerity and depth of feeling are displayed in this dynamic writing. Absence of adornments discloses that Brahms exercised self-control, never allowing his impetuous nature to give full vent to passion and emotion.

The signature maintains the same size as the body of the writing, although he makes an ornamental annex to the last letter. In this graphic expression his whole enthusiasm is pictured.

HECTOR BERLIOZ

French romanticism springs from a different source than that of German, for it reflects the revolutionary tendency. Berlioz, Bizet,

Cesar Franck, all write in the melodic tradition of Schumann. The chief exponent of French romanticism is Hector Berlioz. He is the veritable Proteus. His writing changes like the colors of the sea and sky. The heavy down strokes in this writing display great will power. Berlioz's high artistic aspiration is shown in the upper part of the letters, which climb into the sphere of creative imagination. We see charm and harmony here, and the rapid tempo discloses enthusiasm.

The writing moves on to the right in a dynamic way; some finals are turned, and others are pointed. These graphic traits mean sarcasm and strong critical faculty. The wavy t-bars bespeak his well-developed sense of humor. The warm, pasty pressure shows that his nature is impressionable and acutely responsive to impressions in ways beyond description.

CHARLES GOUNOD

Charles Gounod's excellent taste and refined critical sense are revealed by the rapid and graceful movements of his script. His was

a spirit of culture! The beautiful bows in this dynamic writing bespeak a combination of dramatic and lyric sense.

CESAR FRANCK

Cesar Franck's script is from the year 1871, when he was fifty-one years old. It is taken from his most creative period. The threadlike connection reveals the writer's ability to adapt himself to conditions and his tremendous facility for improvisation. Threadlike connection often reflects unreliability of character. This is not

so in this case, because the threadlike connection is coupled with a certain amount of legibility. It must therefore be interpreted in a positive sense, as he has the ability to adapt his music to various styles of composition according to necessity.

In spite of its tremendous speed, there is no confusion in this writing. The spacing between words and lines is even, denoting the same clarity which Franck employed in the structure of his compositions.

GEORGES BIZET

Georges Bizet's writing pictures his verve and his creative dramatic imagination in the determined way with which these lines are set to paper. The form level is superior, and there is great sense

of proportion in the straight lower loops and in the whole arrangement of this script, revealing Bizet's strong sense of drama. Some pointed finals, although short, reflect his cynicism.

Very impressive is Bizet's signature. The writer was well aware of his important place in the world of music. The whole writing is ascending, emphasizing his vigor and his artistic temperament.

14.

The Modern Period

RICHARD WAGNER

In order to understand Richard Wagner we must return to the earlier romantic period in Germany. Wagner, a true son of the revolution, unites in his compositions a happy blend of romantic and classical ideas.

His handwriting reveals this union, expressing his logical, convincing transition from one emotional complex to the other in the new and unique style of his writing. He reverts to the old style in some letters, such as the small "d" and "f."

The two specimens of Wagner's handwriting written in French date from the time of his exile in Switzerland. His creative power is shown in the original capitals, which climb into the upper sphere, as well as in the determination with which he forms his letters.

Wagner's sensuality is disclosed in the enlarged lower loops. The upward trend in the ascending lines, especially of the second writing, is a symptom exhibiting his fine understanding coupled with a flair of mysticism.

Exaltation is expressed in the dashing t-bars, showing that his enthusiasm carries him out of this world. The elegant formation of letters reveals his cultural background.

Wagner's well-developed critical sense is reflected in the pointed endings. His superhuman will power, strong enough to conquer all obstacles, is shown in the heavy and even pressure.

This highly dynamic writing, with its great perspective, is an emphatic expression of Wagner's great dramatic genius.

GIUSEPPE VERDI

Giuseppe Verdi's writing is from the year 1858. Without any doubt Verdi is the greatest dramatic genius musically, that Italy has produced. This ever-changing script, showing great perspective, heavy pressure and tremendous speed, reveals Verdi's unerring theatrical instinct and his passionate nature.

Strong vitality and energy are expressed in the warm shading of the pressure. The angular connections, together with the heavi-

ness of the strokes, seem so filled with the power of expression that they appear to break and scratch the paper. His will power can almost be identified with obstinacy.

The high climbing letters symbolize his inspiration and creative imagination. There is a strong emotional expression and warm-hearted nature shown in some of the garland connections.

His signature is original, circling itself around his name with a beautiful flourish, revealing his wit and his great sense of humor.

RICHARD STRAUSS

Richard Strauss, often humorously called the second Richard, certainly is not only a child of his age, but he is also a great genius following the voice within him.

This script is a true picture of his fascinating personality, expressing brilliance, wit, and an enthusiasm for intellectual subtlety, all of which are revealed in the wavering underlining and high climbing letters. Although the letters reach the upper sphere, they show neither religious fervor nor metaphysical background. In

GARMISCH
ZOEPPRITZSTR. 42

Strauss' upper zone the letters are mere extensions and express a personal mannerism.

The whole script discloses that the writer is a realist of magnificent vitality. The heavy horizontal pressure can be considered displaced pressure, revealing his interest in sexual abnormalities and Freudian complexes as shown in some of his compositions, such as *Salome and Electra.*

In the constructive disconnections and superior form level, Strauss' delight in fantastic experiences are reflected.

These few lines display great perspective, representing the creative originality of Strauss' extraordinary genius.

CLAUDE DEBUSSY

The French composer Claude Debussy repeats in his writing the impressionistic period in music with which he is closely identified. Some features of romanticism are still visible in his sensitivity

toward color, which takes the form of light and shade in his script. The diminutive elegance of this writing is to be contributed to the writer's musical impression, as well as to the influence of French impressionistic painting and poetry. There is no passion or deep feeling expressed in this script—only lyric refinement. The effect of distance, the perspective, displayed in the script, which we call the third dimension, reveals his irrefutable genius.

MAURICE RAVEL

Here is a certain affinity in the characters, expression, and conception of Debussy and Ravel. While we observe a certain effeminate delicacy in Debussy's writing, we see in Ravel a stronger rhythmic backbone, a more realistic, forceful and masculine type of script, disclosed by the heavy pressure which is mostly in the horizontal strokes. This script displays great creative power; all the letters are formed with a special sense of clarity, in addition to an obvious curved surface which shows the third dimension. The bold-

ness of his musical compositions, the ardor and temperament, the fertility of his creative power are displayed in many letters and especially in the graceful capital letter "S" in the second line. Innumerable musical symbols are present in this script, visible even to the layman who never has investigated such a writing. The evenness of the pressure shows his tremendous energy and unique sense of musical color.

The upper zone predominates, but the lower is well-developed, showing the balance of his vital reality.

DARIUS MILHAUD

The script of Darius Milhaud, like his music, tends to be more dramatic than lyric. The abandonment of his isolated initials and the verve of his writing as a whole are parallel to the vital facility of

his composition. The swift stroke over his signature is an outward manifestation of his general assurance of his place in modern time as a revolutionary composer.

EDWARD MACDOWELL

In Edward MacDowell's harmonious script we find a good example of the musician's sensitivity and the lyric soul of an artist. The even spacing and beautiful arrangement of the entire writing reveal his aesthetic sense, while the graceful flourishes reflect his talent for the fine arts. The fluency and dynamic of this script show his vitality of mind, and the originality of letter forms mirrors his creative powers. The writing as a whole reflect the inherent purity of his personality; his perseverance and vitality are shown in the firm pressure. His sense of musical color is obvious in the lights arid shades of his writing.

It seems evident that the writer of these lines is a fine, lyric tone poet rather than a dramatic composer. The writing is simple and clear, lacking in artificial effects; letters growing upward into the upper zone reveal a spirit rising above the heaviness of the world. This is a true expression of the composer's aesthetic sense of harmony.

PAUL HINDEMITH

Paul Hindemith's handwriting displays much modern originality in the simplified, but original letter forms. The steadiness of this script shows the composer's sense for form and the definite, invariable trend of his musical ideas. The structure of all the letters has a strict perspicuity; there is no futile stroke or movement, everything is limited to mere necessity. The beautiful letter "P" in his signature is elevated into the higher sphere, also the capital letter

"E" at the beginning. The spacing is wide in comparison to the size of letters, both horizontal and vertical, but mathematically equal, revealing the writer's objective lucidity of ideas. This spacing, in addition to the heavy pressure on horizontal strokes, gives the writing a great perspective, called the third dimension.

The rhythmical and fluent writing pictures the fertility of his musical ideas, and the small and distinct letters with angular con-

nections betray the composer's facility and skill in playing different instruments with ease. The emotional aspect is hardly evident in this clear and simplified writing, revealing that Hindemith does not care much for the emotional expression, but rather for clarity and variety of form. His neo-classical trend is obvious in the simple way of writing, void of any romantic impulse. This very simplicity also shows the mastery of his individual style of composition, as well as the modesty of his personality. The wavy "u" signs and some comma-like i-dots betray this composer's creative and conspicuous sense of humor.

BÉLA BARTÒK

The late Béla Bartòk's script displays extraordinary dynamic and perspective. The tempo is very fast and fluent, so much so that it seems the composer can hardly follow fast enough to put his creative ideas on paper. The very smallness of these letters reveals his love for working out even the minutest details.

The pressure is mostly on horizontal strokes and very heavy; disclosing that the writer has sublimated his passionate nature in

favor of his creative work. Little time seems to be left for his personal needs—they are even neglected (threadlike connections).

There is an intuitive and highly sensitive personality expressed in these delicate lines: some heavy pressure on falling downstrokes reveals a nature given to depression. However, a good amount of humor will make up for occasional depressive states (long wavy t-bars). It is the handwriting of a genius who shows leader quality and who is able to give direction to his musical expression.

PAUL CRESTON

Paul Creston, an American contemporary composer, is one of the most representative creators of modern American music.

In his sample of handwriting we observe simplifications of letters. However, we also notice the great difference in these simplifications in comparison with the script of Hindemith. While in Hindemith's writing there is angularity in the connecting small letters we see garlands in Creston's script, revealing his quality of deep feeling.

Being of Italian descent, there is warmth expressed by the shaded pressure. As in many previous handwritings of composers,

Dear Mª Marwse —

As one who has collected specimens of

for many years, I am happy to su:

I hope you will have a greet de

probing into my innermost self

With all good wishes.

Paul Creston

we observe that the pressure is mostly on the horizontal strokes, revealing that the writer's emotions are sublimated and transposed into his musical expression. We can find here his sense for melody, although in a modern style, as well as his love for *bel canto.*

The individual shaping of letters, in addition to many constructive disconnections, gives evidence of his creative ability and imaginative powers. The change of slant discloses his versatility and easy adaptation to everything new and progressive.

NORMAN DELLO JOIO

Norman dello Joio's handwriting reveals the writer's boldness and originality in his musical creations by the highly individual letter formations and the self-assured way of putting these lines on paper. The slight change of slant is a sign of versatility in composing.

A person who writes such a graceful, quick, fluent and rhythmical script must possess a quick, ingenious and inventive mind, well

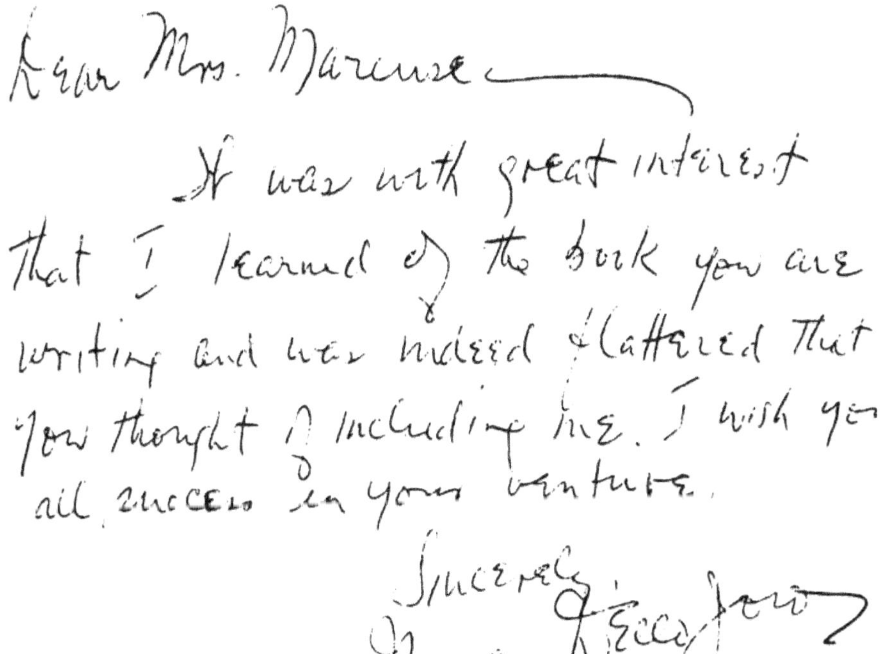
Dear Mrs. Marcuse—

It was with great interest that I learned of the book you are writing and was indeed flattered that you thought of including me. I wish you all success in your venture.

Sincerely,
Norman Dello Joio

equipped to hold a place in the mainstream of modern American musical life.

On the other hand, there is simplicity and modesty expressed in the simplified, legible and well-defined small letters, showing that simplicity is the core of his creative roots. The very dynamic script and third dimension mirror a uniquely personal vision and the abundance of ideas.

WILLIAM SAMUEL BARBER

With Samuel Barber we will conclude our examination of modern American composers.

Some of the high-climbing, somewhat embellished capitals, particularly in his signature, reveal the essentially romantic com-

You may use my name

Advisory Committee and

Sincerely yours,

Samuel Barber

poser, although the well-defined small letters disclose that Samuel Barber can use the conventional idiom of the late nineteenth century naturally and feelingly.

The modernity of this small script discloses him as a child of this time who has been exposed to diverse influences.

The very firm strokes of the pen with heavy, even pressure, in addition to the high form level, reveal the strength of his personality and his talent, which has made it possible to integrate these influences into his music.

As a whole, this clear and well-proportioned script shows that the composer has succeeded in arriving at a convincing synthesis of his talent, and has found a style unity distinctly his own.

BIBLIOGRAPHY

Abrahamson: *Crime and the Human Mind,* Columbia University Press.

Adler, Alfred: *The Science of Living.* Greenberg.

Allport and Vernon: *Studies of Expressive Movements.* Macmillan.

Baldi, Camillo: *Trattato come da una letter a misciva si conoscono la natura e la qualità del scrittore.*

Beers, Clifford W. A.: *A Mind That Found Itself.* Doubleday.

Burnham, William H.: *The Normal Mind.* Appleton-Century.

Crépieux-Jamin, J.: *L'écriture et le Caractère.*

Eliasberg, Wladimir: "Political Graphology" in *Journal of Psychology,* XVI (1943).

Erlenmeyer, D. Die Schrift: *Grundzuege ihrer Physiologie und Pathologie.*

Freud, *Anna: Introduction to Psycho-Analysis for Teachers.*

Jacoby, Hans: *Analysis of Handwriting Self-Knowledge Through Handwriting.*

Jung, Carl: *Humanity in Search of a Soul.*

Klages, Ludwig: *Handschrift und Charakter. Die Grundlagen der Charakterkunde.*

Leichtentritt, Hugo: *Music, History, and Ideas.* Harvard University Press, 1938.

Marcuse, Irene: *Applied Graphology.* Macoy.

Meyer, Georg: *Die wissenschaftlichen Grundlagen der Graphologie.*

Michon, J. H.: *La Méthode Pratique de Graphologie.*

Morgan, J. J. B.: *Keeping A Sound Mind.*

Murphy, Gardner, Lois B. Newcomb T. N.: *Experimental Social Psychology.* Harper.

Osborn, Albert S.: *Questioned Documents.*

Pophal, Rudolf: *Die Handschrift als Gehirnschrift.*

Preyer, Wilhelm: *Zur Psychologie des Schreibens.*

Pulver, Max: *Symbolik der Handschrift Trieb und Verbrechen in der Handschrift.*

Roback, A. A.: *Personality in Theory and Practice.* Sci-Art.

Roman, Klara: *Handwriting.* Pantheon.

Saudek, Robert: *Psychology of Handwriting.*
    Experiments with Handwriting.
Sonnemann, Ulrich: *Handwriting Analysis.* Grune & Stratten.
Teltscher, H. O.: *Handwriting, The Key to Successful Living.*
Victor, Frank: *Handwriting, A Personality Projection.* Thomas.
Wolff, Werner: *Diagram of the Unconscious.* Grune & Stratten.

I N D E X   O F   M U S I C I A N S

Index

Also available from:
www.sunvillagepublications.com

PSYCHOGRAPHOLOGY

How To Uncover The Secrets In Handwriting
For Self-Understanding and Personal Power

Robert Holder

Your Personality
In Handwriting

Lyn Brook

CPSIA information can be obtained
at www.ICGtesting.com
Printed in the USA
LVOW02s0401210317
527896LV00003B/18/P

9 781438 255828